O9-AHV-866

PQ   11839
3902
W3
Warwick
The long journey

PQ   11839
3902
W3
Warwick
The long journey

DATE	ISSUED TO

CHESAPEAKE COLLEGE
WYE MILLS, MARYLAND

 PRINTED IN U.S.A.

THE LONG JOURNEY

LITERARY THEMES OF FRENCH CANADA

UNIVERSITY OF TORONTO ROMANCE SERIES / 12

THE LONG JOURNEY

Literary Themes
of French Canada

JACK WARWICK

UNIVERSITY OF TORONTO PRESS

© UNIVERSITY OF TORONTO PRESS 1968

PRINTED IN CANADA

UNIVERSITY OF TORONTO ROMANCE SERIES

1 / Guido Cavalcanti's Theory of Love, *by* J. E. SHAW

2 / Aspects of Racinian Tragedy, *by* JOHN C. LAPP

3 / The Idea of Decadence in French Literature, 1830–1900, *by* A. E. CARTER

4 / Le Roman de Renart dans la littérature française et dans les littératures étrangères au moyen âge, *par* JOHN FLINN

5 / Henry Céard : Idéaliste détrompé, *par* RONALD FRAZEE

6 / La Chronique de Robert de Clari : Etude de la langue et du style, *par* P. E. DEMBOWSKI

7 / Zola before the *Rougon-Macquart*, *by* JOHN C. LAPP

8 / The Idea of Art as Propaganda in France, 1750–1799: A Study in the History of Ideas, *by* J. A. LEITH

9 / Marivaux, *by* E. J. H. GREENE

10 / Sondages, 1830–1848 : Romanciers français secondaires, *par* JOHN S. WOOD

11 / The Sixth Sense: Individualism in French Poetry, 1686–1760, *by* ROBERT FINCH

12 / The Long Journey: Literary Themes of French Canada, *by* JACK WARWICK

11839

PREFACE

Start at the beginning, go on to the end, and then stop: what a wonderfully ironic piece of advice! But a writer of criticism should not be grieved to find that there is no beginning or end. New literary creations and criticism are the best proof that his chosen subject is still full of life. Such is the case with the present work, and it is with both satisfaction and regret that I have to mention the omission of relevant material published since I wrote most of what follows. At the time, *Cul-de-sac* and *La Montagne secrète* were still quite recent, and seemed to bring the theme of the journey to a temporary halt. One rounded off the moral sense of the subject, while the other explained its meaning to the artist. In fact, however, journeys within my definition still appear from time to time, and there is no neat chronological pattern into which their significance might fit.

Félix-Antoine Savard's play, *La Dalle des morts* (1965) continues the traditional feeling for the *pays d'en haut* as a necessary but disruptive part of the national heritage. Savard's Preface states very plainly that his use of historical material expresses a psychological forest, in which there lurk nostalgic memories of the *coureurs de bois*, the purity of Canadian nature, and love of the true freedom. His notes indicate that the *pays d'en haut* he envisages, complete with *coureurs de bois*, start on the Ottawa River. This is a surprising use of these terms by a living author, and shows how the frontiers of time and space continue to give way to the living legend.

Marcel Godin's novel, *Ce Maudit Soleil* (1965), adds to the other side of the legend. His brutal account of lumber camp life contains elements which are essentially those of the hard savage: an authenticity, a vitality and a rashness which arouse admiration and misgivings in equal proportion. The hero painfully learns self-knowledge in this almost elemental setting, but appreciates it only when traditional lumberjack life is doomed by the ineluctable advance of civilization. The bearers of this civilization are Displaced Persons from Europe, a bold and challenging device for a Canadian author to choose. Because these men were obliged, irrespective of their former occupations, to spend a period of adaptation in the backwoods, Godin's hero is suddenly confronted by men as literate and sensitive as himself, and his unresolved feelings are dispersed in ambiguous relief. The novel thus conforms to the pattern of the journey as quest, described in my Chapter Four.

Transcontinental journeys such as Jean-Jules Richard's *Journal d'un hobo* (1960) are to be distinguished from the categories I have established, both by the profile of the journey itself and by the use of political innuendo. Jacques Godbout has since added to this type his *Le Couteau sur la table* (1965). At the time of writing I did not find enough material to form a meaningful category, but this may now be possible and could lead to interesting comparison with Jack Kerouac's use of the transcontinental journey.

Other interesting variants on the *pays d'en haut*, such as Gabrielle Roy's Prairie writings, have been either omitted or barely mentioned in the interests of brevity and simplicity. Their relation to the themes under discussion is marginal, and it is not the object of this book to assess their undisputed charm. The works of Maurice Constantin-Weyer, Georges Bugnet, and Marie Le Franc, French writers working Canada, have been completely omitted. They did not seem to demand inclusion, either by mere weight of national fact, or by complete identity with a theme. Louis Hémon's unique role in French-Canadian literature, on the other hand, makes him quite indispensable for any account of the pioneer myth, and essential to my definitions of pseudo-geographical regions. The inclusion of Harry Bernard presents a slight inconsistency, since he was born in England, and *Les Jours sont longs* has not had the influence of a *Maria Chapdelaine*. On the other hand, his early and permanent settlement in Canada appears to have exposed him to predominantly French-Canadian influences, and the novel is the best one specifically set in the James Bay region, as well as containing a forest type who amplifies our understanding of related types. Other omissions concern the almost countless missionary tales and other minor works which help constitute the tradition, particularly by popularizing a legendary geography and a traveller hero. These have been of great value to me in formulating the general perspective of the subject.

The decision to include or omit is not necessarily a value judgment. For the nineteenth century, particularly, it seemed less important to be exhaustive than to analyse material which sheds light on the whole tradition. Thus, Joseph-Charles Taché is treated at length, whereas relevant portions of Louis Fréchette's prose are not even mentioned, and his poems are cited briefly to illustrate a point without attempting to do him justice on his own grounds. I have preferred to expand on even one small aspect of a novel like *Poussière sur la ville*. For although its references to the *pays d'en haut* may seem slight, they are intense because the novel is intense, powerful because the tradition they draw on is powerful, and central to Langevin's world because they show the way from Madeleine Dubois to Pierre Dupas. If my argument has thrown light not only on Langevin, but also on Yves Thériault and Gabrielle Roy, I feel I have done French-Canadian literature a greater service than I could by holding the balance between a Taché and a Fréchette. I hope I am even justified in giving a certain prominence to Georges Dugas, a less accomplished writer than either of these.

Finding a beginning is just as difficult as making a selection or an end. The Jesuit Relations are so extensive, and bring with them so many questions about French education and Spanish colonial policy, that a thorough treatment would have to be quite disproportionate. I have preferred a mere mention. Even Sagard needs to be placed in a much wider context, as I hope to show elsewhere. Meanwhile, my views on him and on Champlain have changed, though not in any way that would affect the position of the *Grand Voyage* in this book. Whatever it meant to the Franciscans in their Paris convent, his account of the *pays d'en haut* is for us the fullest early expression of a reaction which was shared, and has continued to be shared, in modified forms. The vocabulary and concepts relating to *libertins*, noble savages, and *voyageurs* are at present far from being a closed chapter. Even the apparently innocuous expression "mangeur de lard," for instance, demands more than the traditional explanation which I hesitantly accepted. Professor M. A. Screech, in his *Marot évangélique* (1967), maintains that the expression already had a proverbial sense in the Middle Ages. Widened, in the first place, to refer to any meat eaten during Lent, it was extended to any kind of criminal on the run. Although other evidence is wanting to show that this sense was still alive in nineteenth-century Canada, it does fit the picture of new recruits to the canoe trade better than their supposed yearning for bacon. Furthermore, the invention of this latter explanation is itself suspect, and possibly one more item in the general effort to whitewash the reputation of the *voyageurs*.

This book has been written for a wider than specialist public. I have, therefore, thought it best to include long quotations rather than brief references to texts which may not be generally familiar or easily available. Similarly, most of the poems mentioned can be found in the anthologies listed in the bibliography; although these are out of print they can usually be found in libraries. I have also reduced as far as possible the system of footnotes, so that they might not be cumbersome or tedious. I hope this will not inconvenience specialist readers, and that they will sympathize with my desire to enlarge, if I can, the circle of interest in French-Canadian literature.

This work has been published with the help of a grant from the Humanities Research Council of Canada using funds provided by the Canada Council, and a grant from the Publications Fund of the University of Toronto Press.

J. W.

The University of Western Ontario

CONTENTS

THE LONG JOURNEY

LITERARY THEMES OF FRENCH CANADA

Introduction

If anything is well known about French-Canadian literature, it is the image of Maria Chapdelaine. Many French Canadians think it is much too well known and spreads an impression which, though containing some truth, is not by any means the whole truth. Perhaps if Louis Hémon's novel were really well read, instead of just widely known, it would be less misleading. As things are, it is too easy to think of Jean-Baptiste as an unquestioning peasant like Maria's father and husband, tied to the soil of Peribonka and to the eternal values it is supposed to embody. With him the only expression of adventure is pioneering, which consists essentially of reproducing the same static pattern in different places. That this image is inadequate must be obvious to everyone, yet it has been supported by many French-Canadian writers and by the official canons of taste. We are led to wonder whether all French-Canadian literature is bucolic, and how French Canadians react to the obvious tokens of adventure and non-conformity.

The North is well known to the English reading public as a region of adventure and challenge, and we naturally ask ourselves how it impinges on the French-Canadian consciousness, how it is treated in the French literature of Canada. A cursory examination reveals that there is a considerable body of writing concerned with the North. In the first place, because of real human contact with frontier regions, there is a tradition comparable with farming. The *voyageur*, a picturesque social type, has become a legendary figure who appears to dominate the *pays d'en haut*, a region which can be defined mainly by reference to the fur trade of the early nineteenth century. In the second place, this literary and oral tradition is quite clearly associated with a spirit of adventure such as we might expect. However, the sense of challenge found in traditional writing on this topic is neither clear nor predictable. In many cases it is reconciled—or muddled, depending on the skill of the writer—with the static ideal of Samuel Chapdelaine. That is to say, the basic values of the writer's society finally go unchallenged. In other cases, a writer seems to proclaim a spirit of liberty which ought to be in direct collision with accepted values. We are usually disappointed of such a collision. Thus, the French-Canadian literary tradition of the North appears at first sight to arise from popular awareness and oral tradition, to be colourful and adventurous, but, beyond that, rather unsatisfactory.

There are good reasons why the enquiry should be pursued further. The decline of the agricultural myth in literature, and the deeper change of attitude that goes with this decline, have released some of the forces which were previously muffled. The rise of a new critical and even revolutionary spirit poses the question, has French Canada a rebel tradition of its own, or are the new writers completely dependent on an intellectual lead from France? Then there is the "Northern" literature itself; for all it is muddled or displaced, the spirit of challenge is there. It needs to be defined and evaluated; the apparent inconsistencies need to be related to the whole tradition if there is one, to discover whether they are a random or a systematic occurrence. All of this demands a fuller examination of representative material, to situate this field of literary interest historically, to define some of its key terms such as geography, social types and literary figures, and to seek characteristic patterns which may not have been evident at first sight.

Modern sources readily indicate that the whole feeling about the *pays d'en haut* is connected with semi-legendary folk types including the lumberjack, the *voyageur* and the *coureur de bois*. This suggests a continuous tradition from the *ancien régime*, as indeed does the survival of the expression "pays d'en haut" itself. A fresh examination of the early uses of these terms in French confirms that they were associated with a more or less admirable outlaw. Their vestigial connotation is of an open challenge to authority, and an escape from the controls to which the French colony was subjected. With this in mind, we must enlarge the scope of our enquiry. Novels set in regions which are not particularly northern, but containing rebel figures who are literally outsiders to organized society and its values, must also be considered, particularly if their settings resemble more distant forest regions.

This in turn leads to a geographical survey. The steady advance of civilization obviously means that the *pays d'en haut* have been continually receding. Once they began at Montreal, whereas now the term is mostly used as an historical concept denoting a region beyond Lake Superior which ceased to exist when Manitoba became a province of Canada. The term "North" continues to be used, with the same elasticity as its predecessor. However fluid these concepts of popular geography may be, we must attempt to penetrate their vagueness, to see whether any meaningful patterns emerge. In the literature associated with the North, it is in fact possible to establish divisions which relate types of feeling to areas on the map of North America. There is considerable overlapping between them, but even this has its meaning.

The regions thus established are commonly associated with the French-Canadian missionary movement. Both the original French colonies and Lower Canada in the nineteenth century made much of the hardships and courage which went into penetrating the untamed parts of the continent. They both connected religious conversion with the spread of a higher civilization, and both had a very rigid idea of the ethic they were spreading in the name of that civilization. Clearly, this association of the *pays d'en haut* is diametrically opposed to the rebel spirit. It has to be accounted for, both to assess its own contribution to literature and to bring a clearer understanding to the confusion of values which we have already noted.

Once definitions are established, it is possible to look for the larger values of literature. Has the Northern inspiration made any real contribution to the most outstanding French-Canadian works? Does an understanding of this complex set of associations add to our appreciation of them? Is the North a parochial obsession, or does it transcend its natural limits with emotions analogous, say, to those with which Jack London's grim wastes or Boris Pasternak's bleak deserts have assumed a poetic value for readers physically quite remote from them?

In the survey portion of the work which follows, I hope that I have established that there is such a thing as a coherent body of French-Canadian literature concerned with what must be loosely called the North. Although geography is a necessary part of it, it is not the major interest, and is extremely flexible. Consequently, it is by no means specious to include works where the physical notion of the North is reduced to a small vestige, but where the spirit of this elusive North is strong. It is in such works as these that the real literary potential of the matter is fully developed, and the superficial local colour discarded. Nevertheless, these works owe more than is at first evident to the continuous tradition from which they have emerged. They all contain a searching dialogue between absolute values and a questioning spirit, which echoes the basic dialogue of all "Northern" literature. A knowledge of the traditional associations of the "North" intensifies our appreciation of that dialogue within individual works. The major elements of Canada's northern syndrome have deeper affinities. The exalted revelation contained in a journey, the sense of wonder in various kinds of nature, the nostalgia for natural man,[1] and the urge to build empires are all common experiences recorded in literature and sometime termed archetypal. These, and not the location of Long Sault, are the real core of the "North" as a literary phenomenon. Finally, and most important both within French-Canadian literature and in its connection with wider human experience, there is the endless sense of quest. The literary imagination, when it turns to the North, is restless and questioning, and in search of something it cannot find by keeping still.

Readers of John Buchan's *Sick Heart River* are familiar with the search for regeneration in the North, where lost men find themselves and the sick are made whole. The hero of Hugh MacLennan's *The Watch that Ends the Night* is a man who still

[1]There is no simple way of delineating the complex variety of meanings associated with the words "nature" and "natural man," nor even the different extents to which individual authors using them are subscribing to mythical significances. Of these the principal which concern us here are: (1) a harmonious cosmic force most visible in uncultivated scenery, but possibly capable of giving man peace if he would/could surrender to it; (2) a kind of man imagined to be free from the constraints and artificialities of civilized society; and (3) the Christian views of man in relation to the Fall.

finds himself in the memory of his native forest, and his great healing powers are in some way due to the crude vitality he brought from it to Montreal. The lone voyager is a familiar figure among the myth makers of English-Canadian poetry. The themes and images of the North have aroused similar responses in Canadian writers in both English and French. Although it is beyond the scope of this work to make a detailed comparison between them, it may be observed in passing that in both languages the North expresses the feeling of the artist as non-conformist. It may also be added that this association seems particularly strong among French Canadians, emerging as it does in the Franco-American Jack Kerouac who is the plainest example of a *coureur de bois* by inheritance, turned writer by circumstance.

The rebel spirit is the side of French-Canadian literature which is most interesting today, and which should be put in the balance with the innocent resignation of Peribonka. Its success is not simply due to its coincidence with current fashions in French fiction, though this undoubtedly plays its part. The savage sincerity of André Langevin, the ironic conviction of Gabrielle Roy and the reforming vigour of Yves Thériault are the outcome of an authentic Canadian experience. There is some unity in their protest, even more in the "Northern" expressions they have all found. This gives some answer to the difficult question of national cultural identity in French-Canadian literature.

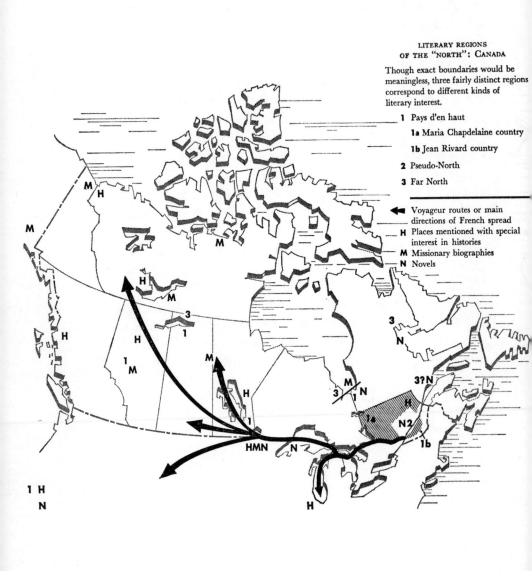

LITERARY REGIONS
OF THE "NORTH": CANADA

Though exact boundaries would be
meaningless, three fairly distinct regions
correspond to different kinds of
literary interest.

1 Pays d'en haut

    1a Maria Chapdelaine country

    1b Jean Rivard country

2 Pseudo-North

3 Far North

⟵ Voyageur routes or main
    directions of French spread
H Places mentioned with special
    interest in histories
M Missionary biographies
N Novels

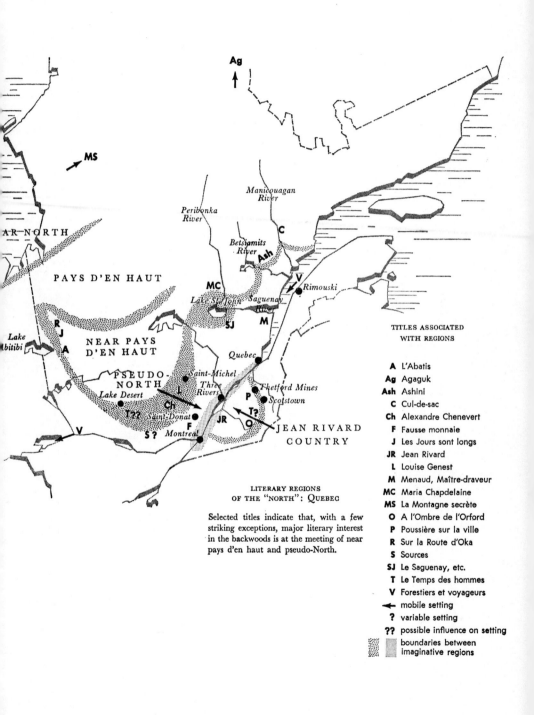

Ag

MS

FAR-NORTH

PAYS D'EN HAUT

Manicouagan River

Peribonka River

C

Betsiamits River
Ash

V

MC

Lake St-John *Saguenay*   Rimouski

SJ

M

Lake Abitibi

R
J
A

NEAR PAYS
D'EN HAUT

Quebec

PSEUDO-
NORTH   *Saint-Michel*

Lake Desert   *Three Rivers*   *Thetford Mines*

Ch   L   P   *Scotstown*

T??   *Saint-Donat*   T?

F   JR   O

V   S?   *Montreal*   JEAN RIVARD
COUNTRY

LITERARY REGIONS
OF THE "NORTH": QUEBEC

Selected titles indicate that, with a few
striking exceptions, major literary interest
in the backwoods is at the meeting of near
pays d'en haut and pseudo-North.

TITLES ASSOCIATED
WITH REGIONS

A   L'Abatis
Ag   Agaguk
Ash Ashini
C   Cul-de-sac
Ch   Alexandre Chenevert
F   Fausse monnaie
J   Les Jours sont longs
JR   Jean Rivard
L   Louise Genest
M   Menaud, Maître-draveur
MC   Maria Chapdelaine
MS   La Montagne secrète
O   A l'Ombre de l'Orford
P   Poussière sur la ville
R   Sur la Route d'Oka
S   Sources
SJ   Le Saguenay, etc.
T   Le Temps des hommes
V   Forestiers et voyageurs
←   mobile setting
?   variable setting
??   possible influence on setting
░░   boundaries between
     imaginative regions

CHAPTER ONE

Historical Background
of the *Pays d'en haut*

It is a truism that any new set of human conditions experienced on a large scale produces its own vocabulary. However, both the words supplied and the new concepts involve older usages and concepts. Moreover, a phrase once coined will often outlive the conditions which produced it, thus prolonging the concept it once denoted into a half-life of varied connotations. This has been the case with "les pays d'en haut" and allied vocabulary used by the Frenchmen who lived in Canada during the formative period of the colony. The geography of the new continent and its economic potential produced some fairly precise technical terms. One of the first was "coureur de bois" (later "coureur des bois" but now commonly restored to its earlier form). This denoted a new socio-economic type. Later came "les pays d'en haut," meaning areas upstream from the colony, and later still "voyageur négociant" (rapidly reduced to "voyageur") meaning another kind of occupational type. All these three terms survived the conditions in which their exact use made sense because they had built up a set of associations and attitudes. They can even be used today, though their archaism would normally now be felt. On the other hand, their associations and attitudes have survived, in some cases being attached to other words such as "le Nord," meaning a vague region which seems to be the imaginative centre of the whole group.

The expression "pays d'en haut" appears to be of popular origin. It arises from common knowledge of a country whose chief feature, evident on all early maps, is its great waterways. It simply meant the lands reached by going up the canoe routes.

This was one pole of the Canadian world. The other was France, reached by going downstream from the colonies on the St. Lawrence. Downstream led to the absolute monarch, upstream led to possibilities without bounds.

An emotional connotation grew with the term itself. An anonymous critic of the government, writing in February, 1712, appears to be the first user in recorded documents of the expression *d'en haut*. He talks of *les nations d'en haut* and *les missions d'en haut*.[1] What he has to say about them is very plainly that they are a haven of tolerated licence:

Pour Lors les Gouverneurs et Intendants se prevallants des deffences contre ceux qu'il leur plust ne laisserent plus faire les commerces deffendus qu'a ceux qui les faisoient pour eux et de leur part, qui marchant la teste levée non seulement avec licence, mais mesme avec authorité le libertinage vint a tel Excés que le zele des peres jesuistes ne le pouvant supporter, Le Pere De Careil Superieur des missions d'en haut aima mieux brusler leur chapelle et se retirer a Quebec que d'estre temoin occulaire et perpetuel des profanations et horribles sacrileges qui se commettoient journellement jusque au pied des autels et pendant la celebration de nos mysteres. [C 11 A, 33, 267]

The earliest official and recorded use of the complete phrase *pays d'en haut* is in a joint report of Ramezay, the interim Governor, and Bégon, his *Intendant*, dated November 7th, 1715. Ramezay was fully aware of the *libertinage* of the forest and of its economic basis. He was equally aware of the military and commercial importance of these regions to the French empire in North America. He knew exactly the dilemma which all the Governors faced: the life of the colony was inextricably linked with the expansive vigour of the *pays d'en haut*, which was at the same time a constant menace to royal authority. So he comments on a proposal for dealing with the menace of the Fox Indians:

[Le Sieur de Lignery] propose de faire monter le printems prochain a Michilimakinak cent sauvages de nos domiciliers et deux cent françois ces derniers a leur depens pour se joindre aux françois et aux sauvages qui sont dans les pa[ïs] d en hault et de les faire

---

[1]*Archives coloniales, Canada, correspondance générale* (Paris), C 11 A, volume 33, pages 270 & 267, respectively. Subsequent reference to these archives will be shown, whenever convenient, by the abbreviation C 11 A, followed by the volume number and the page number.

assembler a l isle de Manitoualin dans le lac huron pour de la alle[r] attaquer les Renards dans leur fort en accordant aux françois qui seront employes a cette Expediti[on] le commerce Exclusif des païs d'en hault pendant deux ans.

Ce projet ne nous a pas paru convenable conoissant que ceux qui ont fait cette proposition au Sr de Lignery ne peuvent avoir d'autres veues que celle de profiter seuls pendant ces deux Années du commerce du païs d'en hault. [C 11 A, 35, 18]

Ramezay's own plan was to send men out under royal control and on royal pay. This was a bold proposal, if we may judge from the general tone of the colonial archives, which abound in excellent schemes that were to cost the king nothing.

An observation of the historian François-Xavier Garneau indicates that the expression had passed into regular usage by about 1725, when Louis XV himself made a marginal note on a memoir, emphasizing the importance of the *pays d'en haut* for trade. The three uses we have mentioned, occurring within two decades, indicate the three main facets of the *pays d'en haut*: liberty, ambiguity and empire. The existence of a recognized expression, with these connotations as well as a geographical sense, is the culmination of attitudes developed during the seventeenth century. Once the phrase had been coined and accepted, it flourished and remained with all its clouded associations.

The *libertinage* of the *pays d'en haut* had been known for some time under various names. The men who sought it were essentially outside the planned progress of the colony, although they were essential to exploration and thus indirectly profitable to the king. Accordingly, measures were resolved against them but never properly executed. This created an interesting new commercial condition. Their illegal activities usually needed connivence in high places, which the irregularly paid government officers secretly gave, to repair their private fortunes. Expeditions condoned in this way could be in the public interest, by spreading French influence and exploration, without drawing on the royal coffers. To Jean Talon, whose basic honesty is seldom questioned, such duplicity may have seemed the best practicable course. In two memoranda of the same date, 2nd November, 1671, he announces contradictory policies. One offers to explore for minerals by means of a party which would pay for itself by trading in beaver pelts as it went. The other mentions marriage as a means of making young men settle down to tilling the land instead of going off into the woods. Under subsequent governments this split attitude simply became more corrupt and led to more impossible situations.

Who were the *libertins* and what kind of men were they? Over this, the official documents draw a veil, but it is not a very thick one. Talon was a wise civil servant, who sent softened reports home. He referred merely to "plusieurs faineants" (C 11 A, 3, 176). In his own edicts he was much more firm, and called them by their name:

Deffences de vendre prêter ou fournir aucunes marchandises, Boissons ou denrées aux Coureurs de bois, ny d'acheter d'Eux aucunes pelleteries, du 27 Septembre 1672. [C 11, A, 3, 223]

After this document, the phrase "coureur de bois" became very current in official reports. Frontenac, less discreet than Talon, used it frequently and frankly:

Le nombre des coureurs de bois augmente tous les jours,

and:

Ce que le roy m'ordonne de faire aux coureurs de bois m'embarrasse presques autant, puisque ceux sur qui je me puis reposer pour les faire chastier sont les premiers qui les appuient, et qui les protegent. [C 11 A, 4, 26 & 51]

The *coureur de bois*, being neither bureaucratic nor literary, leaves no succinct picture of himself. He is recorded only by his detractors, sincere or hypocritical. However, some characteristics are clear. He was not just an ordinary vagabond. His entry into the language under a name of his own denotes a certain importance in the collective consciousness. The phrase itself suggests a popular origin, and we can be certain, because of the great government concern to prevent the *habitants* from going off to join them, that these men occupied a large place in the popular imagination.

It is also certain that the *coureurs de bois* had existed as long as anyone could remember. Every officer reporting on them makes it clear that the *coureurs de bois* problem was rife before his own appointment. Before the clear emergence of the new term, the words *truchement* and *libertin* are found, expressing two different facets of what was certainly the same social type. *Truchement*, from the same Arabic word as the English "dragoman," was the normal word for an interpreter-guide in the seventeenth century. *Interprète* also existed, but was used mainly in connection with written works and critical interpretations of the classics. A *truchement* was a practical fellow of low social status, like Molière's Covielle. Indeed, he was probably more of a Covielle than was good for the leaders who relied on him for effective contact with the new country.

On the question of *libertinage* the Canadian experience throws some light. Major French writers in the seventeenth century used the word *libertin* to mean either a man free from religious authority or one who has overthrown all rules. Thus, Covielle is a *libertin*, in that he overthrows paternal order in favour of a natural order. Some writers went further, by assuming that lewd and disorderly behaviour would follow automatically. Gabriel Sagard, for instance, establishes a loose link between *libertins* and *athées et charnels*, in speaking of the French interpreters. He also equates fun with freedom in speaking of the Hurons, when he says: "ils sont libertins et ne demandent qu'a ioüer et se donner du bon temps."[2] This, together with the documents quoted in this chapter, suggests that writers on Canada anticipated what is normally regarded as a later use of the word *libertin*.[3] The reason is undoubtedly that the colony presented an extreme form of the conflict between authority and freedom. In this conflict, freedom was very graphically represented by the *coureurs de bois* and *truchements*.

Etienne Brûlé is both the model and first recorded example of these interpreter-guides. As a youth he was sent by Samuel de Champlain into the forests to mix with the Indians. There, faithful

[2]Gabriel Sagard, *Le Grand Voyage du pays des Hurons*, 3rd ed. with English translation as *The Long Journey to the Country of the Hurons* (Toronto: The Champlain Society, 1939), 339; M 175. [The second page reference here and throughout this study is to the first edition, ed. D. Moreau, Paris, 1632.]

[3]None of the seventeenth-century dictionaries clearly show this sense, which Littré associates with Jean-Jacques Rousseau. Henri Berr's succinct listing of the major early meanings shows that the notion of debauchery was present but not very real in most writers of Sagard's time (*Du scepticisme de Gassendi*. Paris: Albin Michel, 1960, 15).

to his orders, he learned their language, their skills, their customs and their methods of trade. He would have been a perfect agent for the French had he been content to remain, with all this knowledge, a servant of Champlain, whose intention was to have a network of such men to assist the spread of Christian law and French order. However, Brûlé learned too much from his hosts, and was condemned by Champlain as an unworthy representative of Christianity. He was also known to Sagard, who travelled with him and wrote a little about the interpreters. It appears that these youths became partly assimilated to the life which they had been sent to observe, mainly because they enjoyed its unaccustomed liberties. This was an important part of the heritage which they left to the *coureurs de bois* proper. These also adopted the Indian mode of life at the same time as becoming guides, traders, trappers and freebooters.

It is easy to see how such men must have struck the other inhabitants of the colony, but harder to say exactly what their life was like. Scandalized missionaries threw up their hands in horror, rather than describe the profanities and excesses. Governors and the like had other reasons for saying little, since they had to avoid revealing their trade relations with the outlaws. While it was widely believed that the *coureurs de bois* could get rich quickly, it was also suggested that this was an illusion because their protectors took everything. The most reliable comments indicate that the real attraction was liberty itself. The Intendant Duchesneau complained that "ils s'accoutumoient à une vie faineante & vagabonde qu'ils ne pouvoient plus quitter."[4] Governor De la Barre wrote scornfully of independent groups leaving Montreal to live as they pleased. He was particularly hostile to Cavelier de la Salle, whose head had turned while he was away in the bush:

il s'escarte de moy dans la pensée d'attirer des habitans a plus de 500 Lieuës d'icy dans le milieu des terres pour tascher de se faire un Royaume Imaginaire en desbauchant tous les Banqueroutiers & faineans de ce pays. [C 11 A, 6, 137]

The Imaginary Kingdom of Liberty has never failed to attract men. In this case, it seemed to possess the flower of Canada's

[4]*Arch. col.* C 11 A, 5, 42.

manhood. "Ils sont les plus capables de faire valloir & deffendre la collonie," said Duchesneau, and repeated that,

ceux qui pouvoient seuls la faire valloir estans jeunes et ayant la force de travailler abandonnoient leurs femmes & leurs enfans la culture des terres, et le soing d'eslever des bestiaux. [C 11 A, 5, 42]

Apparently unable to understand the appeal of such an escapade and such disobedience, he sought explanations. One was Frontenac, who encouraged them. But he also found a more curious explanation—the spirit of the land. The simple peasants who were willing to devote themselves to the land were, he maintained, better off than in France, but,

comme les Esprits de ce pays prennent aisement l essort ci qu'ils ont beaucoup de l'humeur Sauvage qui est Légere Inconstante & Ennemie d'un travail assidu, voyant la liberté qu'on prend si hardiment de courir les bois Ils se debauchent avec les autres et vont chercher des pelletries pour avoir moien de vivre sans rien faire & c'est d'ou vient que les terres ne se deffrischent pas. [C 11 A, 5, 51]

It would be easy to dismiss this as the work of a civil servant justifying himself to his superiors. All of Duchesneau's reports are written in that spirit, and he finds many other good reasons for failing to curb the wayward. Yet his hypothesis is supported by the testimony of others. Frontenac, as Governor general, invoked a similar explanation to justify his high-handed treatment of François-Marie Perrot, the governor of Montreal. Perrot was arrested for practising, through the *coureurs de bois*, the illegal trade which Frontenac wanted for himself. Eventually they were reconciled, and joined forces to contravene the monopoly they were officially supposed to uphold. Meanwhile, Frontenac's false ingenuousness seems more than apposite:

A moins d'une exemple et d'une punition très sévère il ne faut point esperer contenir icy les gens dans la soumission & l'obeissance, puis qu'il n'y a jamais eu peut estre de païs, ou l'authorité soit si mal establie. [C 11 A, 4, 51]

And De la Barre commented on his visit to Montreal: "J'ay reconnu que tous les peuples de ce quartier sont peu sousmis a l'obeissance et Connoissent peu la justice" (C 11 A, 6, 138).

The Jesuit historian Charlevoix, who had no administrative failures to hide, seems to come closer to a spirit of the land, but has more confidence in the idea of assimilation to the character of the Indians:

On diroit que l'air, qu'on respire dans ce vaste Continent, y contribuë, mais l'exemple & la fréquentation de ses Habitans naturels, qui mettent tout leur bonheur dans la liberté & l'indépendance sont plus que suffisans pour former ce caractere.[5]

These commentators on the character of the early Canadians were able to give accurate and well delineated descriptions of human phenomena, but we feel obliged to examine their scientific perspectives in the light of modern psychology.

C. G. Jung tentatively concludes his discussion of the problem of the spirit of the earth with remarks to the effect that transplanted Europeans are observed to acquire, in very few generations, some of the characteristics of the original possessors of their new land. He mentions the phenomenon of "going bush" in Australia, the rigid fight against negro assimilation in South Africa, the Indian hero-motive in North America.[6] Jung's suggestion as it stands in "Mind and the Earth" is very incomplete, yet it does offer some explanation of the repeated observations of French colonizers in Canada. Something aroused in the settlers a feeling for unbridled liberty, which became one of their dominant characteristics. At the same time, contrary forces sought to maintain in them an equally extreme sense of law and order, a spirit of absolute obedience sometimes attached to the idea of family and farm as essentials of the Christian life. Between these two poles the character of a new people developed, and was later to find its way into literature composed under very different historical conditions.

The Jungian mechanism is not incompatible with more tangible explanations of the attraction of the *pays d'en haut*. The economic advantages of illegal trade, even if they proved illusory, must have seemed real enough in the imagination of both *seigneur* and *habitant*, who saw their estates growing surely but very slowly. Their life was monotonous and frugal, whereas that of the *coureurs de bois* seemed rich and colourful; did not Duches-

---

[5]Charlevoix, *Histoire et description generale de la Nouvelle France* (Paris: Nyon fils, 1744), III, 172.

[6]C. G. Jung, "Mind and the Earth," in *Contributions to Analytical Psychology* (London & New York: Routledge, 1928).

neau himself report that they claimed the flower of the colony's manhood, and decked themselves in finery? Life in the colony, too, was restricted by Church and state interference, which affected the highest and the most humble. The most substantial definition we can give to the word *libertin* as it appears in this context is "one who escapes official supervision." The many ordinances against such escape are evidence enough of the controls that were to be shaken off.

While the *coureur de bois* seemed like a dashing hero to the frugal *habitant*, he also inspired abhorrence in the right-minded. His own notorious licence was bad enough, but worse than that was the ruinous effect of the liquor trade on the Indians. The occupation of the *pays d'en haut* by the *libertins* was opposed to the whole purpose of the colony, which was supposed to confer the benefits of Christian civilization on the savages. In spite of obvious discrepancies, this was not just a hollow password; some people meant it.

The idea of the civilizing mission is too well known to need a detailed account here. A few remarks will suffice to show how different views of the new country could be. Champlain is probably the plainest and certainly the most influential representative of the view that civilizing is a one-way communication. Knowledge of the natives was an important attribute of his perfect mariner, but we infer that it was mainly an aid to navigation. It was easy to see, he reminded his readers frequently, that the *sauvages* were not really good, although at times they might seem to be. Their life was really bestial, because they had no law and no established manner of worshipping God. Some had even no idea of God. However, there was hope of conversion, and this was the principal concern of the French king, who, raising his eyes to heaven rather than gazing upon the earth, would support the colony for that end. Champlain frequently refers to agriculture as an essential part of this policy, partly because it would supply the Europeans with food but also because it would demonstrate to these disorderly brutes the proper way to live. There is a passage, much revised in succeeding editions of the *Voyages*, where he states that the Indians themselves often requested a colony for that reason. The revisions show all too clearly that this was not a distinct memory of an actual conversation, but

19

rather the author's own synthesis of many dialogues in which he did more talking than listening. Flattery probably played a great part in such conversations as actually took place, for the Indians were on the look out for powerful allies, and the interpreters were men of little integrity. It would be easy to echo his own views and send him away satisfied: "leurs discours me sembloient d'un bon sens naturel."[7]

Following Champlain's line of thought, inland exploration like the original settlement was for the sake of "leur reduction en la cognoissance de Dieu." In this process, French family life and agriculture were to be infallible instruments, like the ones which had brought him successfully across the ocean. His *truchements*, as we have seen, saw something very different in the *pays d'en haut*. We have no positive evidence of what they thought about the society they were abandoning, but they obviously did not find it so unquestionably right as their captain.

For the Jesuits in particular, conflicting attitudes to the civilizing process helped to prepare an intellectual crisis. Of course they were also aiming at conversion, but for reasons partly political, partly doctrinal and partly pedagogical, they had a more lenient view of the children of nature than Champlain. The insidious theory of the "good savage" had various fortunes in France between Lescarbot and Fénelon. With its Virgilian reminiscences, it made most progress among the scholarly Jesuits. Lafitau, finally, expressed views which seem quite incompatible with the doctrine of original sin.[8] The edifice of evangelization was threatened from both sides: the pure savage was being corrupted by the *libertins*, and Christians were being converted by the unregenerate savage.

Still, the Jesuits did not give up their ambitions for the *pays d'en haut*. These represented the scene of future conversions, a fulfilment. In the face of English and Protestant rivalry, this fulfilment would always be linked with the problem of national penetration. The Jesuit order itself was very active in exploration, supplying cartographers and martyrs. The *pays d'en haut* were

[7]*The Works of Samuel de Champlain* (Toronto: The Champlain Society, 1922–1935), IV, 321. Cf. *Ibid.*, III, 146.

[8]Gilbert Chinard, "Influence des récits de voyage sur la philosophie de J.-J. Rousseau," *Publications of the Modern Language Association*, XXVI, 2 (New Series XIX, 2) (1911), 476–95.

the land of heroes as well as outlaws, priests as well as *libertins*. Indeed it was often hard to maintain the distinction—one could turn into the other at any moment. Most of the great explorers were caught in this dilemma. Their expeditions had to be financed by incidental trade. While they were away, their enemies found ears willing to listen to calumny, imaginations disposed to think of them as *coureurs de bois* or profiteers using discovery as a pretext. The *pays d'en haut* were, in every sense, an area of moral confusion.

It is in this context that the *coureurs de bois* were officially condemned but openly tolerated, even admired. Most of the principal persons had an interest in unofficial trade. So, in spite of everything, had the colony, because it was strategically necessary for the French to maintain relations with the Indians of the *pays d'en haut*. The *coureurs de bois* were a necessary part of the colony's expansive vitality. It was still possible to maintain a religious sense of direction, although it was partly hypocritical. The *pays d'en haut* were a symbol both of crusade and of viable opposition to theocracy.

Because in fact they were not simply outlaws, the men of the forest were not isolated from the stable population of New France. Awareness of the *pays d'en haut* was considerable, and the mentality which is associated with them was common in the colony. Some of her native sons were inspired to become great explorers, and enough took to living in the woods to provoke laws restricting the use of canoes. The canoe is at once a symbol and a means for the independent spirit which Charlevoix and others noted in the Canadian character. This was, naturally enough, most pronounced among the *coureurs de bois* themselves, and evidence from all sides shows that their reckless spirit became a cause of growing concern to the administration. Francis Parkman gives a glowing picture of them as colourful rakes swaggering through Montreal on frequent visits, or revelling in their own forts in the *pays d'en haut*. Lionel Groulx sees them as "une maladie, un chancre" and "francs révoltés" endangering "la vocation agricole."[9]

After the death of Louis XIV there is evidence of a relaxed

[9]Lionel Groulx, *Histoire du Canada français*, 2nd ed. (Montreal: Action nationale, 1951), I, 204, II, 193, I, 110.

attitude towards the problems of the *pays d'en haut*. It is beyond
the scope of this work to examine the cause of these changes.
However, with them we note the more frequent appearance of
the word *voyageur*. What it denotes is not new. All the expeditions from those of Jacques Cartier on had needed men to paddle
and portage their canoes. There had grown up a tradition of
skill and endurance in these matters. Men were willing to serve
in teams under the leadership of a trader or explorer with some
official status. It is in this respect that they differ from the *coureur
de bois*, with whom, however, they have many characteristics in
common.

It is not possible to generalize with certainty on how genuine
the difference was. It is notorious that most of the *coureurs de
bois* had trade relations with the government officers who were
supposed to suppress them. The significance of this new term in
government reports is that the bush ranger was more acceptable.
The new name gave him a place in the organized world, and
made him more palatable to higher authority.

The term seems to have started as *voyageur négociant*, indicat-
ing a man who went to trade with the Indians in their own
areas. It may have been free of the pejorative tone of *coureur de
bois*. The anonymous complaint of 1712 (quoted on p. 12 above)
uses it in a completely neutral sense in its reference to a control
point at Michillimakinak "ou tous les voyageurs negociants ou
caneaux soient obliges de se rendre." It axiomatically uses
coureur de bois in a pejorative sense in its angry marginal note on
the Governor's appointing "Ceranye coureur de bois toute sa vie"
as ambassador to the Indians of the upper country.[10] However,
early references indicate that in fact there was not necessarily any
difference in behaviour. Ramezay's first mention of *voyageurs* as
such was to report in 1712 that they had taken to the bush:

C'est avec un extreme chagrin monseigneur que j'ay l'honneur de
vous informer de la desertion de douze voyageurs quy se sont
Evadés cette année. [C 11 A, 33, 151]

He further associates them with *coureurs de bois* by mentioning
the amnesty of the previous year, which was specifically intended
to allow *coureurs de bois* to return to the colony.

[10]*Arch. col.* C 11 A, volume 33, 269–70.

On the other hand, it is not long after this report that the *voyageurs* are mentioned as an established trade needing more royal support in order not to be driven into criminal activities. The same Ramezay, in 1715, asked for authority to grant more canoe permits, as the only way of meeting English competition for the trade of the inland Indians. He wanted:

des permissions pour 25 Canots au moins d'autant que quinse ne suffiroient pas pour employer le nombre de voyageurs qui sont dans la Colonie lesquels n'ayant que cette profession resteroient toute leur vie dans les païs d'en hault refractaires aux ordres du Roy plus tost que d'abandonner ce genre de vie. [C11 A, 35, 21]

Ramezay, alternately defending the interests of the *voyageurs* and expressing displeasure at their disobedience, shows that whatever new concept there was, the same dual problem persisted. Their freedom was both a necessity and a nuisance. The adoption of the term *voyageur* represents a partially successful attempt to be realistic about independent trade, to bring it more into line with the development of the colony. Ramezay, in trying to absorb the *coureur de bois* into lawful channels, recognized a real principle of growth in the people he was governing.

As the influence of established society progressed, the word *coureur de bois* became less used. Further, *voyageur* itself underwent a change of usage. It eventually came to be used almost exclusively as a synonym of *engagé*, a man who offered his services to traders with capital. A hierarchy was formed among the men who had previously refused to conform to social order. A whole vocabulary grew with it. The *bourgeois, commis, hivernant* and *mangeur de lard* all knew their places. The *mangeur de lard* was so named because he was supposed not to have lost his craving for the staple food of the *habitant*; that is to say, he was a new recruit employed on the lower reaches of the trade routes.[11] He seems to have accepted the convention which did not allow him to wear the *ceinture fléchée*, the dazzling insignia of the seasoned *voyageurs*. The *hivernant* was an important development of the ever lengthening trade routes: he did not return to Canada for the winter, as the men on the lower reaches did. He was therefore likely to spend the rest of his life in the *pays d'en haut*. The *commis* and the *bourgeois* were responsible

[11]But see also my Preface, x.

officials of the company, the latter being in some cases the financier and head of a small company.

All of this seems like a considerable toning down of the reckless *libertin* spirit which had thwarted Champlain's attempts to build a team of useful interpreter-guides. Nevertheless, the *voyageur* did not lose all the aura of liberty associated with his forerunners. The social order he had built was not the same as that of the colony, and he still had ample opportunities to exercise his taste for independence, or even lawlessness. The great adventure of exploration continued, notably with the La Verendrye family, though the pressures of war curtailed this activity for a time. The *pays d'en haut* themselves must have seemed to grow both in wonder and possibilities, as the Prairies, like a sea of grass teeming with buffalo and other prizes, were increasingly known.

Voyageur life seems to have been substantially unchanged by the Conquest, after which its growth was encouraged. The tradition of special skills and knowledge was as quickly fostered by the British authorities as it had been opposed by the French. The Governor, Sir Guy Carleton, reported in March, 1768:

Your Lordship will readily perceive the advantage of such Discoveries, and how difficult attempts to explore unknown Parts must prove to the English, unless we avail ourselves of the knowledge of the Canadians, who are well acquainted with the Country, the Language and Manners of the Natives.[12]

This opinion was general, and the new trading companies of Montreal employed French-Canadian *voyageurs*. The fact has been extensively mentioned by subsequent writers, and became a point of pride in the *voyageur* legend. The tradition continued until new methods and new economic factors brought about its decline around 1840. Alexandre-Antonin Taché, a missionary, stated that his journey from Montreal to the *pays d'en haut* in a bark canoe was the last of its kind. That was in 1845. The canoe continued for some time to be the summer method of transport between points within the *pays d'en haut*.

All through this period the main *pays d'en haut* were the North-West parts of the country, which meant the Prairies until

[12]Quoted in *Report on Canadian Archives, 1886* by Douglas Brymner (Ottawa, 1887), clxxi.

Confederation made new designations necessary. This fact probably helped create the important present-day confusion between "North" and "pays d'en haut." The older term could presumably still apply to upstream areas closer to home, that is to say, the Laurentians and the Eastern Townships. These, however, appear to have attracted comparatively little interest in the first half of the nineteenth century. The adventurous spirits found their outlet in the land of the *voyageurs*, the buffalo, the Iroquois and the great trading companies. The presence of these made communications possible over great distances, and popular knowledge of the region was augmented by their policy of seeking French-Canadian personnel. Despite the predominance of English or Scottish employers, the *pays d'en haut* continued to offer an escape from British colonial rule as they had from French colonial rule and from some of Canada's new economic problems.

At the behest of the Hudson's Bay Company a few French-Canadian priests founded a post at Red River to care for the Roman Catholic personnel and to spread the faith among the unbaptized. Inevitably, as the movement grew in strength, writers grew from it, and were drawn by the idea that their work was a direct continuation of the mission handed to Samuel de Champlain by His Very Christian Majesty.

Real similarities were not lacking. The new missionaries suffered privation, isolation, and eventually, with the murder of Fathers Rouvière and Leroux in 1913, martyrdom. Even if they had trade routes to follow, they were still explorers in the important functions of providing accurate reports of the land, its resources, its native populations, their life, language and character. Rivalry with the English interlopers was still a constant problem, though modified by the new situation. And everywhere that he travelled in company, the missionary found himself with *voyageurs* like the ones who had been on all the great expeditions.

Although the *ancien régime* produced some notorious hypocrisy, this was always limited by practical considerations. These no longer counted when men like Francois-Xavier Garneau set about re-discovering the glory of the French people of North America. They were able to echo official statements of policy as they found them, and state blandly that the aim of discovery was the conversion of the Indians.

Clearly, in the middle of the nineteenth century, it was no longer realistic for French Canadians to think of spreading the rule of the *roi-soleil* as of old. Yet there were still outlets for dreams of empire. Missionary work increased in the area which had been discovered by the last French explorers. There were still virgin forests to be cleared. Above all, there was literature, the new type of conquest which had been invented by the national historian: writers could finish the task of their forefathers by encouraging colonization and French Catholic values. These three outlets for expansive vigour were easily confused with each other, which is why a body of writing grew up around the *pays d'en haut*.

At the same time, social changes associated with the *voyageurs* are noticeable. A new race of Métis was born of *voyageurs* and their Indian spouses. Like their mothers, they were nomads who lived on buffalo hunting. From their fathers most of them inherited the French language and the Roman Catholic religion. The new missionary movement which was reaching them coincided with agricultural settlements, fostered notably by Selkirk. The forces of society again encroached on the freedom of the *pays d'en haut*.

The conflict of order and independence emerged in a new form. It became mixed with other conflicts, particularly those between languages and religions. French presence in the *pays d'en haut* did not maintain its predominance. A curious illustration is the life of Alexandre Beaubien, the first native resident of Chicago. During his long life there grew, from the settlement where he was born, a city of two million inhabitants. A-G Morice records this in his Dictionary, which is a proud monument to the achievements of French Canadians in the North-West, yet he can evidently find nothing to show that Beaubien took any active part in this remarkable development. Nevertheless, the simultaneous growth of the missionary movement and of a French-speaking population seemed like a fine example of the spread of French cultural influence, a triumph over the Anglo-Protestant rival. For religious and linguistic conflicts became the major ones, and are still having serious repercussions in the educational system of Manitoba. Once the economic conflicts between hunters and settlers lost their meaning, history could be interpreted in rival ethnic claims, like that of Morice's introduction:

Traiteurs et trappeurs, coureurs de bois et explorateurs y étaient à l'origine, et demeurèrent longtemps, presque tous de notre nationalité. ... Mon but a été de faire ressortir l'action de l'élément français dans ces vastes régions et, par corrélation, y affirmer les droits qui lui sont acquis.[13]

It is not clear when the term *rayonnement* was adopted to denote this historical theory: Larousse notes similar figurative uses by Hugo, Gautier and Lamartine, so that its special application in Canada is quite normal. *Rayonnement*, or more fully *le rayonnement français*, denotes the will to expand, to spread all facets of French cultural influence, usually understood in Canada to mean French-Canadian Catholic influence. The Oblate publishers in Montreal changed their name to *Rayonnement* in 1955. This is a full but very tardy recognition of a movement which was implicit a century earlier and has some claims to continuity as far back as Champlain. Its spiritual ancestry in him is best seen in his inflexible will to civilize North America as he knew best, that is to say by acquainting the natives with God and plough, and by curing them of their own obnoxious customs. This attitude was reflected in the nineteenth century not only by historians and writers but also in the actual policy connected with *missionnaires-colonisateurs* like Alexandre-Antonin Taché and Patrice Lacombe.

In serving the ideal of *rayonnement*, many missionaries ran into a serious self-contradiction. The men whose cause they were to champion did not generally conform to the pattern of agricultural civilization the French were supposed to be spreading. The conflict of nomad and settler did not correspond to the conflict of French and English expansions. The implied right to civilize was in agreement with the survivalist view of the French as a superior race, but contradicted the notion of cultural survival as a universal human right. This contradiction did not emerge clearly at the time, because French-Canadian nationalist sentiment was becoming increasingly divorced from the liberal nationalisms of the nineteenth-century revolutions. Nevertheless,

[13]A-G Morice, *Dictionnaire historique des Canadiens et des Métis français de l'Ouest* (Quebec: Laflamme et Proulx, 1908), x.

there were signs of uneasiness in Taché's and Lacombe's efforts to settle the Indians down to farming.

Canada itself was undergoing vital changes, both politically and economically. An accentuated search for national identity idealized, among other things, the *habitant*. The social type on which this idealization is based is the opposite of a *voyageur*: the *habitant* is a traditional farmer who neither moves nor changes. He appears to correspond exactly to the wishes of those who, like Duchesneau, had sought to suppress the *coureurs de bois*. Farming was seriously regarded in the nineteenth century as a means of French survival, just as it had always been advocated as a French civilizing influence. It was a means of making a living without giving in to the Anglo-Saxon commercialism which had become the main source of prosperity. It was also a means of occupying a solid geographical area in which the language, customs and religion of the French would be kept predominant. This is not the place to examine the feasibility of this policy, but we must note that it had severe limitations. Agriculturalism was mostly the dream of men who lived in the cities. To all social problems they had a wonderful answer: pioneering like the distant ancestors. The *défricheur*, or pioneer farmer, would not only maintain the true original values of the nation, he would also extend its boundaries.

In this respect the *défricheur* and the missionary were closely allied, at least in theory. For quite different reasons, the *défricheur* was also connected with the *voyageur* tradition, so that for a while it was possible to see this unlikely trinity united in one image of the frontiersman. Their joint conquests for the cause of Frenchness were, principally, the Laurentians and the Eastern Townships. These two regions, which had always been potential *pays d'en haut* by first definition, saw a real increase in French activities at a time when the main *pays d'en haut*, the Red River and beyond, were passing under another sphere of influence. There was increased missionary activity to the near North, as a result of which the French language was expected to spread.[14]

[14]In the long run this type of *rayonnement* failed. Jacques Henripin, speaking to the Royal Society of Canada in Montreal, 1961, demonstrated the overall tendency towards a decline in the use of French outside the main centres of French-Canadian population. A fact of special relevance here is that the number of Canadian Indians adopting French as their first language

In the second place, pioneering experiments were carried out, notably by Father Antoine Labelle in the Laurentians; settlers lived a genuine frontier life in a clerically directed colony. Finally the rise of lumber camps on the upper Ottawa made great advances after about 1850. Coinciding with the decline of canoe traffic, the vigorous new timber industry attracted many of the old *voyageurs*, plus the sort of men who probably would have become *voyageurs*, and the sons from penurious new farms who needed seasonal employment.

Although the type of work was different, the lumberjacks' life was able to continue the traditions of the *voyageurs*, because it was a corporate masculine life involving a considerable journey away from settled society and offering ample scope for the varied skills of life in the bush. It was also an excellent centre for the transmission of folklore. Men who had served on the canoe runs, such as those known to the journalist Joseph-Charles Taché, seem to have been formative influences. Taché himself, in *Forestiers et voyageurs* (1863), had no hesitation in fusing the two occupational types into one folk type, and obviously thought he knew *voyageur* life at first hand through conversation with its veterans in the lumber camps of Rimouski (another area which thus shares in the *pays d'en haut* tradition).

Literary interest in the North grew along different lines at the end of the century, although some interest in folk traditions continued. The Art for Art's sake movement looked to the landscapes themselves for rare, dazzling beauty, in which human figures such as explorers or Indians were little more than an added pigment in a riot of colour. William Chapman's "L'Aurore boréale" (1903) is a symphony in light and sound, pure of moral or historic doctrines:

> Tout à coup, vers le nord, du vaste horizon pur
> Une rose lueur émerge dans l'azur,
> Et, fluide clavier dont les étranges touches
> Battent de l'aile ainsi que des oiseaux farouches,
> Eparpillant partout des diamants dans l'air,
> Elle envahit le vague océan de l'éther.[15]

---

is negligible, being 1.5 per cent, as against 15.5 per cent adopting English and 83 per cent unchanged.

[15]William Chapman, *Les Aspirations* (Paris: Librairies-imprimeries réunies Motteray, Martinet, 1904), 226.

Finally, Chapman places an ecstatic moose in the foreground, to give the scale of this titanic picture and also to avoid relating our experience of impassive beauty to any human themes. René Chopin, in his descriptive poem "Paysages polaires" (1913), uses dying explorers to the same effect. They are not identified with French history, and the emotion associated with their death is merely a dash of warmth to act as a foil to the icy architecture for which they are dying, as a Mallarmé might for his azure ideal:

> Les fiers Aventuriers, captifs de la banquise,
> En leurs tombeaux de glace à jamais exilés,
> Avaient rêvé que leur gloire s'immortalise:
> Le Pôle comme un Sphinx demeure inviolé.[16]

The Adventure, once freed from the insistent symbols of cross and flag, is asserted as an end in itself, or as an element of impassive beauty. Henceforth it will be possible to have attitudes towards the *pays d'en haut* other than those dictated by the survival tradition. The old equations will be broken by some writers and the independence of outlook which has long lain dormant may return. Paul Morin, with a polished war whoop, revindicates the poet's right to seek beauty in Versailles and points east; his "Mississippi" (1917) is an ironic rejection of the Romantic cult which writers like Fréchette had built round the great French discovery in the interior. It is also a rejection of the poet's own earlier promise to marry his French prosodic skill to Canadian themes ("A Ceux de mon pays," 1911). Yet even in disdaining Canadian topics, he has chosen the right one to express his rebel spirit. The *pays d'en haut* remain a convenient place from which to defy authority.

Escape from authority was a serious matter at the beginning of this century. The taste represented by Camille Roy offered little scope for creative vitality. Literature was to be nationalized both in content and purpose. Amoral art was roundly condemned, and its exponents treated to sardonic or faint praise. It is consistent with this situation that poets seeking to adopt new forms should have found exotic themes to go with them. They sought a renewal by looking out from their "jardins trop

[16]René Chopin, *Le Cœur en exil* (Paris: Georges Crès, 1913), 65.

enclos,"[17] as their own apologist put it. They felt a need to escape because society sought to impose narrow limits on all forms of intellectual activity. To this day there are protests against that form of narrowness, like Carl Dubuc's *Notaire Poupart*, a witty caricature of the Quebec conformist.

At the same time, attitudes and themes made popular about 1860 continued to find new expression. They were helped by the new nationalism in politics, especially after the conscription crisis of the Great War. Patriotic themes were also roused by open conflict with exotic and other anti-traditional writing, in the light of which they now seemed more like venerable ancient traditions than they could have when the *voyageurs* were still alive. Agricultural values and the civilizing mission were restored, and can be found in novels and radio talks to this day. The *pays d'en haut* were frequently involved in this, particularly because of their ambivalence.

Lionel Groulx, more than any other individual writer, brought moral purpose and family heroes back into the foreground. *Notre maître le passé*, which appeared in 1924, is a resynthesis of ancestral vigour. Like François-Xavier Garneau, Groulx gave a great deal of credit to official statements of French policy in Canada, emphasizing the missionary purpose. Seeing a historic truth in missionary activity, he showed the missions of the North-West as a direct continuation of the will of the colonial government; Groulx in fact made them into a direct continuation of the Jesuits of New France, and was responsible for bringing the word "diaspora" into vogue in the context of French civilization in North America.

Notre maître le passé brings the notion of the Christian empire back into a period of vigour. It combines the visionary quality of the patriotic generation with the methodical use of detail. It also establishes a few idiosyncrasies. Describing the life of François de Laval, Groulx not only made him without reserve into the saviour of a tottering colony, but also brought to life a list of personal virtues which were to become recognizable facets of a stock missionary type. Typical of these is the portrayal of Laval as a spiritual man who endured gruelling journeys on

[17]Eugène Seers (pseud. Louis Dantin), *Gloses critiques*, 2ème série (Montreal: Lévesque, 1934), 96.

snowshoes. Conversely, for Dollard des Ormeaux whose physical courage is legendary, there is a little rosary of spiritual features, in which "notre race" and Christian belief seem to be the essential qualities of a hero.

The two main types of ancestor have thus been fused. The warrior is something of a missionary, and the priest something akin to a warrior. The pioneer was not to be forgotten either. Mgr. Taché, the recent hero, was the descendant of both Louis Jolliet the explorer and Louis Hébert, the first ploughman of the colony. The spirit of Montreal is typified by Maisonneuve and Marguerite Bourgeoys rather than by a Governor's report of 4 November, 1683 which said: "l'yvrognerie avec des Excés estranges, Le Vol, Les Recelez, et la Desertion sont les choses ordinaires ausquelles s'exercent 200 Libertins qui sont dans cette isle et aux environs."[18]

The Arctic coast represents the obvious fulfilment of missionary ambitions, and has been the scene of activity as well as a centre of interest throughout the twentieth century. French priests first reached the coastal Eskimos from their posts on Great Slave Lake, so that it is in fact a direct continuation of the movement which started at Red River. However, major changes have obscured that continuity. The character of the region and of its native inhabitants presented a new kind of challenge. The era of Victorian self-righteousness gave way to a new attitude to primitive societies. Methods of travel have changed so drastically that the radiating network of canoe routes is less vital than it was even thirty years ago. But probably there is no greater change than the absence, almost complete, of any colonizing intention. Without settling and farming, there is no supporting influx of the missionary's own civilization, and the old combinations of God and plough have no relevance. Thus the Far North, with its repesentatives of the French presence scattered over a vast area, denotes the end even more than the fulfilment of cultural *rayonnement*. On the other hand, undeveloped regions within the Province, particularly Ungava and the North Shore of the Gulf of St. Lawrence, offer some renewal of expansionism.

Through such modified forms, the *pays d'en haut* continue to be a real force. The North of Quebec Province, the Eastern

[18]De la Barre, in *Arch. col.* C 11 A, 6, 139.

Townships and the Gulf of St. Lawrence were opened surprisingly late. During the Depression of 1930, attempts were made to continue the pioneering colony as a form of progress. New methods in the timber trade did not destroy traditional lumber camp life until even more recently. The Government of Quebec is at present more actively interested than ever in northward expansion, thus taking over from the missionaries an important aspect of *rayonnement*. The missionaries themselves have pushed further and further afield, often with a keen sense of denominational and linguistic rivalry. Thus, in the days of the autonomist state, cultural, political and religious pressures continue to express expansive vigour in much the same way as in earlier periods.

Beside this potential empire is the inheritance left by the *coureur de bois*. He produced no body of thought and no clear picture of himself. His lineage has been complicated and falsified. Nevertheless, there is a feeling of evasion which expresses itself most readily in the concrete image of forest and stream, leading to the unbounded possibilities of the *pays d'en haut* and a rebel spirit which is somehow acceptable. Lionel Groulx, who certainly had no tendency to flatter the *coureurs de bois*, recognized in them a part of a double atavism in the whole national character. When modern writers choose to ask the searching, rebellious questions of their literary works in lumber camps, trappers' shacks or on gruelling journeys, they are continuing an ancient memory as typical of the French Canadian as the obsession of Samuel Chapdelaine.

CHAPTER TWO

The Geography
of the Imagination

The works which have been examined to determine whether
there is a French-Canadian literature of the North vary con-
siderably both in the degree to which they may be associated with
precise places, and in the extent to which those places may be
regarded as northern. There are three reasons for this. One is
that the imagined frontier of civilization has moved at various
times, as settled society has advanced in reality; the extreme case
is that of Montreal, whose independence was once a frontier
problem for Quebec, and which is now the biggest centre of
Canadian society. Secondly, the imagined wilderness does not
necessarily correspond to factual geography; the North, like
home, is where the heart chooses to find it. Thirdly, there is a
collision of vocabulary and concept peculiar to French Canada;
the older concept of the *pays d'en haut* dominates the use of the
newer expression, *le Nord*.

Whichever of the two expressions is used—or felt—its appeal is
to the imagination and includes some of the feelings which history
has associated with it. It is an appeal which can draw on geography without being bound by it. This autonomy has been
noticed in the popular North of both English and French
Canadians. Ringuet talks about "[ce] que les Montréalais appel-
lent 'le Nord,' "[1] and shows that it is about two hours' drive out
of the city. A serious geographer, answering topical questions
about the mineral riches of the North, has to discard the term
because it is too vague:

[1]Philippe Panneton (pseud. Ringuet), *Fausse monnaie* (Montreal: Eds.
Variétés, 1947), 7.

34

To many eastern Canadians "the North" could be anything north of North Bay, which is in latitude south of all the four western provinces. To some western Canadians "the North" is the large provincial area north of Edmonton, Alberta. . . . To many Canadians "the North" and "the Arctic" mean about the same thing.[2]

These qualifications must be borne in mind when we talk about the geographical basis of literary works. Nevertheless, it is possible to relate most Northern literature to a map of the continent, and even to divide that map into regions denoting different images of the "North" which usually correspond to a different kind of interest in it. These regions are the old *pays d'en haut*, the pseudo-North mentioned by Ringuet, and the Far North.

THE *PAYS D'EN HAUT* PROPER

The country upstream from the original colonies constituted the first *pays d'en haut*. River valleys immediately adjacent to the St. Lawrence reach one kind of *pays d'en haut*. Regular *voyageur* routes via the Ottawa River and radiating from the present Winnipeg, constitute the main *pays d'en haut*. Despite simple differences, these two regions are in one emotional category. They are felt to be the scene of vigorous French-Canadian expansion, where the virtues and values of the original settlers were nurtured and perpetuated. The Eastern Townships and the Laurentians are areas for real or imagined pioneering, while what used to be the North West is *voyageur* country. Both geographical regions were in fact being developed during the formative period of French-Canadian literature.

The area round Lake St. John became a haven of special predilection, doubtless because it was not directly affected by English presence. Arthur Buies, who was associated with Father Labelle in the colonization of the Upper Saguenay, recorded how a dual feeling about the region arose among the general public in the late nineteenth century. Lake St. John, he tells us, had always been legendary and mysterious, isolated in the northern mountains. His work was to break that legend, to convert the

[2]J. Lewis Robinson, "Arctic Resources," *The Beaver*, Spring 1959, 9.

region into farmland, to persuade people that it was pleasant, fertile and peaceful:

Il y a cinquante ans à peine, personne n'aurait osé croire qu'on pût seulement se rendre jusqu'au lac Saint-Jean; c'était tellement loin dans le nord! Le pays qui l'entourait ne pouvait être que la demeure des animaux à fourrures et, seuls, les Indiens étaient regardés comme pouvant se hasarder dans ces sombres retraites.[3]

Whatever the facts, this was the accepted image. Lake St. John clearly belonged in the imagined *pays d'en haut*. Buies converts it in words into a loving virgin mother where freedom, harmony, and security are reconciled:

Cette petite mer intérieure joue *librement* sur un lit incertain que les années l'une après l'autre déplacent . . . les *molles* et *grasses* rives d'une plaine . . . qu'elle a laissée depuis longtemps à nu, après l'avoir *fécondée* pendant des siècles; elle a certaines senteurs *propres* qui traversent l'atmosphère et vont s'exhaler au loin dans les bois et les champs; on la pressent aux *fraîches* bouffées qui s'échappent de son *sein*, . . . [P. 210, italics mine]

It is the co-existence of these two images that makes the region interesting as *Maria Chapdelaine* country.

Felix-Antoine Savard and Léo-Paul Desrosiers are two names associated with the *Maria Chapdelaine* cult. Savard's *Menaud, maître-draveur* is situated between Laurentide Park and La Malbaie, in a region which lyrical descriptions show as the fringe of farm and forest. Its people and their customs are united with the beauty of the land, and opposed to intruders. This feeling of idyllic enclosure is more complete in Desrosiers's *Sources*, set in the country north of Montreal. Like the Peribonka area itself, Desrosiers's ideal farm is bounded by forest and mountains. Desrosiers is echoing an old pastoral dream in his revival of agricultural propaganda. He gives us a picture of young Montrealers stripping the varnish off pine furniture, and invites us to believe that we too can be country folk if we strip off our urban veneer. He fails because he tries to reconcile values which, in his mind at least, are opposed. What the novel really shows is an ineradicable attitude to the Laurentians which survives change, and reappears under various literary or social fashions. Savard goes

[3]Arthur Buies, *Le Saguenay et le bassin du lac Saint-Jean*, 3rd ed. (Quebec: Brousseau, 1896), 209.

further: *L'Abatis* revives the literature of *défrichement*, the clearing of Canadian land. The region is Abitibi, north of the Ottawa Valley, and was in fact uncleared until the author himself went as a *missionnaire-colonisateur*. These two authors have spread the spiritual values of *Maria Chapdelaine* country over the entire middle portion of the province, whose waters flow into the St. Lawrence (see map, p. 8, region 1a). It is a garden of innocence, and guardian of the true Canadian character, a semi-realist pastoral setting.

André Langevin makes an important exception to this image, in *Le Temps des hommes*. This novel could be set in any part of the garden of innocence we have just outlined, but does not find the Providential harmony of traditional writers. The staple industry is pulpwood, and nearby Scottsville is a very small town. Much of the action takes place round a lake called "le Grand Lac Désert." There is a Scotstown near the pulp centre of East Angus in the Eastern Townships (see map, p. 8, region 1b). There is a Lac Désert in a pulpwood area twenty miles from the upper Gatineau. These may have suggested some of the novel to its author. *Le Temps des hommes* is a dramatic search of man and God for each other, so that Langevin finds the same spiritual frontier as others in the vision of man thrusting into the forest. The difference is in his own reaction to it. It is more an inversion of the Providential vision than a departure from it.

Antoine Gérin-Lajoie first claimed interest in the Eastern Townships as an area for pioneering. In *Jean Rivard le défricheur* he showed a heroic conquest of the forest which was in fact still unconquered in 1862 when the novel was written. Courage, industry, fidelity to Church and cultural tradition are all firm values on which a man can build a life for himself and posterity. The region was to be converted into smiling countryside, and the urge to clear it is basically the same as that observed by Louis Hémon at Peribonka. The poet Alfred Desrochers belongs partly to this region. The Mount Orford of his *A l'Ombre de l'Orford* sticks out of the countryside of the upper St. Francis like a granite reminder of all that is rough, hard and brutal in the poet's heredity. In its shade he is able to dream of the pioneering virtues that he has lost. The Calvary-like ascent of his "Désespérance romantique" suggests the same mountain, but here he speaks of going to "quelque bourg du nord." This again indicates that when French Canadians say "le Nord" they may be thinking "en haut"; there is no essential distinction. The Eastern Townships are—or were—*pays d'en haut*. Local expression still designates the valley of the St. Lawrence and its old centres as "en bas," the term used by Gabrielle Roy's Laurentian farmers.[4]

Alexandre-Antonin Taché and Louis-François Laflèche left the mark of the main *pays d'en haut* in literature. The former, spending all his life in the North-West, leaves the best accounts of the region and of the mission work in it. The latter, forced to return to Three Rivers, there formulated his experiences into doctrine. Mgr Taché's *Esquisse du Nord-Ouest* was quickly recognized as the authoritative account of the Prairies, because of its methodical treatment of the topography, vegetation, animal life, and possibilities for settlers. But it contains more than that. It is a loving record of a strange moment in history when civilized men had begotten a race of nomads who were determined to remain free. Gently, and without the support of theoretical determinism, the author indicates a relationship between the land and its Indians and Métis. Together they seem to breathe the very spirit of liberty. His colleague Laflèche, on the other hand, was assertive and dogmatic, viewing the North-West from his eastern pulpit. This vision contains but few shreds of the North-West itself; Laflèche saw a promised land of challenge and reward for his own people, who had the heroic destiny of converting it all.[5] These two different responses to the appeal of the *pays d'en haut* remain an important dichotomy through the rest of its literature.

Mgr Taché also published his mission memoirs, a precedent which has been widely followed since that time. Such works, too numerous to be mentioned individually, have a certain importance. Together with the biographies of other outstanding missionaries, they make up a formidable total of detailed evidence of the French presence. They constitute a possessive network of minutiae radiating across the whole of the *pays d'en haut*.

Other eye-witness writers include the missionaries G. Dugas

[4]Gabrielle Roy, *Alexandre Chenevert* (Montreal: Beauchemin, 1954), 226.

[5]L. Laflèche, *Quelques Considérations sur les rapports de la société civile avec la religion et la famille* (Montreal: Sénécal, 1866), 47–53.

and A-G Morice. The former wrote biographies of two *voyageurs*, and versions of some current legends. The latter compiled a monumental list of French Canadians who spent their lives in the territory, including all social types. Their work brings factual support to the popular idea that French Canadians carried out a collective civilizing mission in this region.

The idea of a missionary movement on a national scale throws light on the histories and historical novels devoted to the region. In *Les Engagés du Grand Portage* Léo-Paul Desrosiers takes the reader on the canoe journey from Lachine to the Lakehead, and thence to posts beyond Great Slave Lake. It follows carefully the routes that were used by the trading companies at the end of the eighteenth century, builds episodes round places with real names (such as Grand Portage itself) and draws their special features into the story. The main journey has the effect of a strong link with Montreal, and the presence of the *voyageurs* keeps up the sentimental link with their homes in Canada.

The further journeys show the vast extent of the *voyageur* empire. Although the idea of spreading a civilizing influence is restricted in this novel, the French presence is felt to be important. It is emphasized that the *voyageurs* made the fur trade physically possible. The same is true of *L'Epopée de la fourrure*, a history by Régine Hubert-Robert, a writer of travel books. Its descriptions carry the reader on a saga through centuries and vastnesses, converging on the North-West and on the last struggles of the great companies. It stresses the ubiquity and unparalleled skill of the *voyageur* and manages to pay homage to the notion of the spiritual mission of the French in North America, in spite of being based on the fur trade.

In *Nord-Sud* Léo-Paul Desrosiers shows the impact of the legend of the *pays d'en haut* on the settled areas of Canada in the nineteenth century. A curious feature of this novel is that the urge to travel is directed towards California, and opposed to the drive to settle in "les Hauts." Yet California is never very precisely envisaged. The adventurous young men in this novel think of the journey in terms of the one they already know, and which their grandfathers knew. The California gold rush seems like an annex of the North-Western fur trade. The real dialogue is not between North and South, but between the two different kinds of *pays d'en haut*, the pioneer's and the *voyageur*'s. In fact, as *L'Epopée de la fourrure* shows, the first Canadian contact with California was through the fur trade, which extended to what is now Astoria.

Nord-Sud is an historian's reconstruction of the moment in the Canadian past when the *pays d'en haut* were most meaningful as a popular legend. Vincent Douaire, the hero, is a returned *voyageur* and the flower of the village manhood. He is as clearly the ancestor of the lumberjacks as he is the descendant of the *coureurs de bois* whom Talon and Duchesneau sought to keep in the colony by means of marriage. He left in pursuit of further adventures because the need to do so lay generations deep within him. He could not face the prospect of settling down to clear a farm, even though it included marriage with the heroine. Since Josephte was attracted by his adventurous spirit, she and most of the village participated indirectly in Vincent's feeling for the forest and for journeys. His personal adventure is therefore a fictional presentation of the basic *pays d'en haut* dialogue: expansion through pioneering versus liberty through the fur trade. Both these possibilities are appreciated by every character in the novel, though some have a strong bias to one side or the other. Some even seem to understand the fatal crux of this dialogue: *rayonnement* depends on the virile principle which tempts the *voyageur* type, as well as on the maternal principle offered in the prospect of marriage and land. The regions envisaged have a very definite human significance which surpasses their geographical precision.

The Prairies are also the scene of Gabrielle Roy's warm, human descriptions of family life, which the author knew as a reality in her own childhood. *La Petite Poule d'Eau, Rue Deschambault* and *La route d'Altamont* show that she is not unaware of the myths of Quebec and the idea of French presence in the West, and contain some interesting variants on them. But the building of such ideas and myths, which is what concerns us here, is more to be found in the Quebec-centred view of the *pays d'en haut*. Later chapters will therefore pay more attention to books like *Forestiers et voyageurs*, where Joseph-Charles Taché links *voyageurs* with men of the forest nearer home, and actually states, in his idealized description, that they always came back home. The village steeple of provincial Quebec becomes a geographical centre, with radii reaching all over the continent. Taché's is a simple hero spreading his Christian influence over the continent he loves.

It is noteworthy that, where a writer is not very insistent on the feeling for Quebec as a fixed centre, the deficiency will often be made up for him by a preface. A. Bernier, for instance, in his 1888 edition of *Vingt Années de missions,* presents the author Alexandre-Antonin Taché as a thoroughly conventional missionary patriot, devoted to furthering the ideals of the land of his birth. The land of his adoption, and the freedom which Mgr Taché loved in it, are obscured by this feeling of higher order, which is denoted by the expression *gesta Dei per Francos.* Similarly, missionaries from France may be claimed as virtual Canadians, in order to maintain the Quebec-centred ideal. On the whole, the *pays d'en haut* are viewed with a very possessive gaze.

THE PSEUDO-NORTH

One of the results of the tendency to emphasize contact between the *pays d'en haut* and the motherland in the Saint-Lawrence valley has been the creation of a land of illusion which has all the epic qualities of the North, without being too far away from civilization. In many cases it is based on a deliberate fusion of heroic and domestic values. This in turn leads to an ironic treatment of heroic aspirations connected with the North. In addition, a near North is sometimes used to contain a dramatic contrast between man in society and man confronting a wider cosmos.

The part of the *pays d'en haut* which we have described as *Maria Chapdelaine* country is the most ambiguous. Hémon's Peribonka serves as the focus of two types of northward urge, that of the woodsman and that of the pioneer. But the reader's view is foreshortened. He is never taken into the woods with François Paradis except to find the dashing lumberjack hero dead. The living northward quest remains only in the combined figure of Samuel Chapdelaine and Eutrope Gagnon, who falls heir to the heroine. With her he inherits the heroic posture of the adventurer, because he is committed to repeating the monotonous adventure of his ancestors.

The theme of conquest through agricultural expansion continues to attract hack writers in the province. Ernest Laforce writes about missionary-colonizers under the stirring title of *Bâtisseurs de pays*. Aimé Carmel sends the penitent "deserter" of *Sur la Route d'Oka* to find terrestrial redemption in a new colony near James Bay. Here the land is cleared, and the traditional pattern of life rebuilt. The North is salvation, provided you go in good company.

In missionary literature there are also signs of an effort to inflate comparatively close missions into heroic distances. Eugène Nadeau, in *Sapier, prêtre de misère*, has a good case for showing that his hero worked in conditions just as challenging as those of the distant North-West. But he overstates it because he feels his readers want feats of exploration. In fact, much of François-Xavier Fafard's career and worthy achievements were south of James Bay, and James Bay itself was not unexplored when he arrived there. Both biography and geography have been strained a little, to make a genuinely arduous life in northern Quebec look like martyrdom in the Arctic.

Ringuet's *Fausse monnaie* makes fun of the same principle on a smaller scale. The area round Rawdon and similar resorts is regarded by Montrealers as the North, a region of beauty and purity. It is distant enough to bear this illusion, near enough to be accessible. It is like a week-end *Petit Trianon*, where French Canadians go to get a nobler, healthier vision of themselves, and to gaze upon God's mountains further to the north. However ephemeral that vision may prove to be, it means something to them at the time.

Ringuet's awareness of the northern myth is everywhere, even in works which are not directed towards it. His disillusion with *Maria Chapdelaine* country appears in *Trente Arpents*. His rejection of the entire history of French explorer heroes is explicit in *Un Monde était leur empire*. Between the two he has tilted at both the near North and the far North, the heroes of the regular winter lumber camps, and those of the great distance.

Roger Lemelin uses the same illusion of strength in the lumber camp in *Pierre le magnifique*. Most of the episodes in Pierre's rise and fall are set in Quebec City, which is Lemelin's territory. However, an excursion into the nearby forest is necessary. It is both a place of evasion from the law, and the proper setting for strong, independent men such as the popular hero should be. In fact this comic hero fails to emulate the strength of the union organizer or the capricious boss through his own incapacity, to which the virile strength of the lumberjacks is a striking foil.

The proximity of forest and society is also used as a theme by André Langevin, Betrand Vac, Yves Thériault, and Harry Bernard. In *Louise Genest* the village has a geographical name, Saint-Michel; it is clearly near there, though the author, Bertrand Vac, adds a note disclaiming exact identity. The farming and hunting area of *Les Jours sont longs* is the most distant of this group, and constitutes a careful regionalist study by Harry Bernard. We are told that it is near James Bay; it appears to be a day's journey from a small town of any consequence, and it is accessible to tourists adventurous enough to want a hunting trip. It is just as concrete in the mind of the author as Saint-Michel is in the mind of Bertrand Vac. This is not true of the village in Yves Thériault's *Le Dompteur d'ours*. However, it obviously belongs in the same family. It is small, reduced to a set of simple principles, isolated in the mountains, close to a forest containing deer and bears. In all these novels there is a man of the forest whose existence poses some kind of challenge to society. The societies and forest types are developed with different degrees of regionalist interest, Thériault's bear tamer being a rootless impostor, and his village almost an abstract of society. It is safe to say of all of them that they are set in or beyond the Laurentians, the better to draw on the anti-social aspect of the literary descendants of the *coureurs de bois*.

A more extreme example of abstraction is to be found in the diary of Saint-Denys Garneau. A fleeting reference shows that he looked north to the Laurentians for his inspiration.[6] They invoked in him the feeling of physical space, its metaphysical suggestion, the tradition of departure and the widest possible idea of departure. They aroused an ancient urge to set out, which the poet connected with his search for perfection. In fact, none of this concrete imagery appears in his poems, though it is subjacent enough for one critic to regard Saint-Denys Garneau as an

[6]Saint-Denys Garneau, *Journal* (Montreal: Beauchemin, 1954), 112.

essentially Nordic poet.[7] The mingling of the concrete *pays d'en haut* with poetic journeys is more evident in Alfred DesRochers, the poet of the Eastern Townships.

Gabrielle Roy's novel, *Alexandre Chenevert*, is in many ways the best illustration of the pseudo-North. In one sense, the hero never really leaves his tentacular Montreal, while in other senses he goes much further than his physical destination near Tremblay Provincial Park. The bewildered victim of modern civilization feels, for a moment, that he is following the traces of explorers and trappers, as well as communing with nature and finding peace and a pastoral prosperity. Myths have their own reality; his health and peace of mind are briefly restored. Without the physical journey to a mythopoeic region, a few hours on the bus to Saint-Donat, the heroic spiritual journey would not have been possible.

THE FAR NORTH

The literature of the pseudo-North suggests a turning away from further adventures, either decadence or sublimation of the zeal which had carried French Canadians into the original *pays d'en haut*. This is not entirely the case, as a large amount of missionary literature of the Far North shows. Yves Thériault adds to the biographies of *voyageurs* an account of Napoléon-Alexandre Comeau's life and prowess on the north shore of the lower St. Lawrence. *Roi de la Côte Nord* is a stirring tale intended for youthful readers, for whom the life of these hard regions has a message. Descriptions and explanations make it clear that this is no pseudo-North; beyond the mouth of the Saguenay, it is really part of the recently untamed Ungava to which the author returns in his novels *Ashini* and *Cul-de-sac*. These are all obvious projections into a fresh geographical area of the type of history and adventure associated with the *pays d'en haut*. The area is down river from Quebec, but north and historically remote. It had no literature before the term "le Nord" began to displace "les pays d'en haut." Thériault, typically, looks to the living part of the tradition and finds its new sources of vigour.

[7]Romain Légaré, *L'Aventure poétique et spirituelle de Saint-Denys Garneau* (Montreal: Fides, 1957), 48.

Yves Thériault also projects onto Eskimos and Indians the old theme of cultural spread and racial conflict. *Agaguk* and *Ashini* deal, respectively, with an Eskimo and an Indian (Montagnais) witnessing the threat which "white" civilization brings to their own people. Though they are not exact anthropological works, these both have fairly precise settings in the North East. The problems of freedom and survival in a particular society are shown in a way that could be understood in any bicultural society. The North and its complex human problems have offered a new outlet for the special French-Canadian understanding of survival.

Probably the most widely known work inspired by the Far North is *Inuk*, the work of a French missionary, Roger Buliard. This is a very thorough account of life in the Coppermine area, starting with the feeling that Eskimos are men, and not just stuff for conversion. It would be a very contentious matter to count this as French-Canadian literature, and we shall not contradict the author's own opinion by doing so. However, it is to be noted that other French-Canadian missionaries count Father Buliard as one of theirs. The human realism of *Inuk* is not beyond the pale of the new generation.

The last works mentioned gain in depth through real understanding of specific Northern peoples. On the other hand, the vague appeal of the North without such a focal point remains a definite force in literature. It is not confined to the science fiction of Florin Laurent's *Erres boréales*, which creates a new French empire in the North. Because of its ethereal splendour, its stern challenge, and above all its loneliness, the Far North excites feelings of wonder which easily enter into literary creations such as those quoted earlier by William Chapman and René Chopin.

Two novels have developed and exploited such a possibility. Gabrielle Roy in *La Montagne secrète* and Yves Thériault in *Cul-de-sac* both use Ungava to form an integral part of the spiritual drama of their protagonists. In both cases the stern landscape, materially observed and described, expresses about the spiritual adventure something which could not be expressed otherwise. In both cases, as man confronts his destiny, the physical reality of surrounding nature is united with his inner reality.

Cul-de-sac deals with a middle-aged engineer who meets truth and death on the Manicouagan. Trapped in a granite crevice, he is utterly alone to face his Maker. Far from being a regionalist novel, this work includes many memories of the engineer's earlier life, scattered across the world. Yet all these memories are somehow consummated in the northern desert, which becomes a lens through which the helpless man is able to look out of his prison onto the universe.

La Montagne secrète is geographical, in that careful account is kept of the places known to an untutored artist who wanders like a *coureur de bois* in search of beauty and fulfilment. The whole of the sparsely occupied North is included in his peregrination and his artistic vision. Flin Flon, the Great Slave Lake, the Mackenzie River, Aklavik, Ungava, the missionaries and the trading posts all have some importance. The intention is clearly to embrace all of the North with its metaphysical connotation, and then transfer it to Paris, a highly stylized Paris regarded only as the artistic capital. In this case Paris is the lens, looking onto the North which is the artist's soul.

RELATIONSHIP OF GEOGRAPHY TO LITERATURE

The material examined shows that there is in French Canada a wide and lasting preoccupation with "the North." Geographically it is a very elastic concept, because its basis in popular thought is dynamic rather than rigid. Nevertheless, we have found three main areas which have been populated by the imagination, if not by the statistical presence of French Canadians. Of these the historic *pays d'en haut* serve as a pivot to the other two, which are the pseudo-North and the Far North.

Each area has a distinct response in literature. From all of them, it emerges plainly that memories and ideals attach to the myth of the *pays d'en haut*. Some writers are able to develop them, using the concrete image as a starting point for their imagination. Others go in the other direction, starting with their historical-political view and seeking to impose it on the virgin land. These are usually inferior writers, though some rise above the common rule. Among the best of the works we have mentioned, the North is a set of symbols and modes of thought which are capable of infinite renewal. They awaken in the writer's mind aspirations of "beyondness," and the best guide to their artistic use is that they must go beyond geography. Yet they must still have an immediacy, a sincerity, which are invariably denoted by "real" northern imagery.

Some of the best works in French-Canadian literature are either included in or contingent upon this topic, because they do in fact combine immediate perception with transcending vision. André Langevin, Yves Thériault, and Gabrielle Roy all hold the reader in tension between their ulterior thoughts and their concrete observation. Alfred DesRochers draws all his originality from the lifelike immediacy of his symbols.

When René Garneau dismissed the possibility of a distinctive northern literature comparable with Canadian painting, he used the formula: "la littérature exige la présence de l'homme."[8] This is irrefutable, but the presence of a North in men is even more critical than the presence of men in the North.

[8]René Garneau, "Du Concept de la littérature au Canada," *La Nouvelle Revue canadienne*, I, 1 (février-mars 1951), 24.

CHAPTER THREE

Empire

Two main views of the *pays d'en haut* emerge from the history and geography of the topic: one regards it as a place for collective expansion and the other as a place for various kinds of private freedom. The literature inspired by the latter view will be discussed in the next chapter. The traditional French-Canadian literature of *rayonnement* and of patriotic heroes must be described and assessed first of all. This is not because it came first; in many important respects the two views have always co-existed and inter-acted. Nevertheless, it will be necessary to regard the literature of emphatic freedom at least in part as a reaction against the tradition considered in this chapter. This tradition may be safely taken to have been dominant in *pays d'en haut* literature from 1860 to 1930, that is to say, within the period when survival was a major factor in French-Canadian literature generally.

The problem of French-Canadian survival in the nineteenth century caused men to look for the roots of the nation's vitality. They were readily inclined to exaggerate such vitality, and to see strong links of continuity where a more detached historian might see tenuous ones. Consequently, they might take as historic truths those official statements of policy concerning Canada which adorn French history but do not explain it. Similarly, the charming letters which the Jesuits sent home to encourage interest in their mission were apt to be taken at face value rather than in relation to the context of their time. Consequently, these materials may be admitted as antecedents of *rayonnement* literature, but only in the sense that they inspired nineteenth-century writers with varying degrees of misunderstanding. It is like the difference between Gothic and College Gothic.

The belief in patriarchal society is a curious and important example. It was, and indeed still is, common to assume that such a society had always been the backbone of the French in Canada. Authors like Philippe Aubert de Gaspé and Lionel Groulx give the impression that they have personally witnessed its decline, and that foreign intrusion is partly to blame. While there is undoubtedly evidence to support this, the following observation by Charlevoix suggests that the age of patriarchy, like the age of chivalry, has always been dead:

Il faudrait, pour faire subsister de si nombreuses familles, qu'on y menât . . . la vie des Patriarches; mais le tems en est passé.[1]

If it was already too late when Charlevoix visited Canada, it seems reasonable to suppose that such a life has always existed more in intention than in fact.

The same distinction has to be considered with regard to early remarks on the *rayonnement* theme, such as the frequent claim that New France was founded for purposes of evangelization. In some minds it probably was, but French-Canadian writers of the nineteenth century enlarged on the rash assumption that this attitude could be attributed to all their ancestors. On the other hand, they were not mistaken in seeing the value of this message for the men of their own generation. Out of the notion that the civilizing role was an historic truth vested in the French Canadians as a people they made an influential literature which may well have been instrumental in their effective resistance to the assimilation recommended by Durham.

Joseph-Charles Taché will be considered here as the main patriotic writer about the *pays d'en haut*. Reference must first be made, however, to the vast amount of *rayonnement* literature which is associated with the nineteenth-century tradition and runs on well into the twentieth century. This includes mission memoirs and pioneering novels. Léo-Paul Desrosiers will be taken as the author who has best continued that tradition in the present century. Possible new departures will be sought in those works of Alain Grandbois and Yves Thériault which are substantially related to the *rayonnement* tradition.

[1]Charlevoix, *Histoire et description generale de la Nouvelle France* (Paris: Nyon fils, 1744), III, 172.

To understand the vision of the *pays d'en haut* created by the generation of 1860, we have to consider three other names, besides that of Joseph Charles Taché. These are Alexandre-Antonin Taché, Louis-François Laflèche and Antoine Gérin-Lajoie. The former two were missionaries to the North-West and eventually bishops, the one of St. Boniface and the other of Three Rivers. Gérin-Lajoie was for most of his life a civil servant and except for a brief attempt at emigration to the United States of America he hardly left the vicinity of Montreal or Ottawa. Taché's journey to the *pays d'en haut* has been mentioned because it marked the end of the long canoe journeys. A decade later, his colleague Laflèche found it easier to return to Montreal by travelling through the northern United States, where he had the revealing experience of meeting French Canadians who had been assimilated to the American melting pot, losing language, faith, and even their French names. All three men were in some way involved in both the doctrines and the realities of *rayonnement*.

Alexandre-Antonin Taché is particularly interesting in the history of *pays d'en haut* literature because in his own attitudes can be seen the clash of the two main views that characterize it. He spent most of his life in the North-West, and his position was basically two-sided. He was a spokesman for the land of his adoption, and especially its *Métis* population; he was an envoy of his land of origin, a civilizer, a bringer of law and order. The former rôle is most evident in his *Esquisse sur le Nord-Ouest* (1869), the latter in his memoirs, *Vingt Années de missions dans le Nord-Ouest de l'Amérique* (1866). This is a more or less perfunctory work compiled from mission records. The *Esquisse* is a thorough geographical description, in which the writer's personal feelings are occasionally to be seen emerging soberly from his objective account. When he tells us that "Le plus grand tort social de nos métis est celui d'être chasseurs,"[2] he is restraining an indignation felt on their behalf. When he writes on their freedom, he is less restrained:

Tout le monde est libre d'aller, de venir, de chasser, de traiter. A part les difficultés matérielles que l'on rencontre en voyageant, il

---

[2]Alexandre-Antonin Taché, *Esquisse sur le Nord-Ouest de l'Amérique* (Montreal: Charles Peyette, 1869), 70.

n'y a pas sous le soleil un pays où l'on jouisse de plus de liberté, et cela malgré l'impression répandue au loin que la compagnie tient le pays dans un demi-état d'esclavage. [P. 44]

When he describes the country, his lyrical flight echoes the same feelings with a positive eloquence, because what he loves in the landscape of the *pays d'en haut* is that it reflects the feeling of freedom of the men who live in it:

Au chasseur de bison, la prairie est un pays à nul autre pareil, c'est là qu'est son empire d'hiver comme d'été; c'est là qu'il éprouve un bonheur véritable à lancer son rapide coursier à la poursuite d'une proie naguère encore si abondante et si facile. C'est là que, sans obstacle pour ainsi dire et sans travail, il trace des routes, franchit des espaces et jouit d'un spectacle souvent grandiose, quoique un peu monotone. [Pp. 9–10]

The missionary's sympathy is with the nomads, if necessary against the forces bent on their destruction.

The same writer, on the other hand, was officially dedicated to encouraging French colonization in the Prairies. He relates the missionary to the pioneer by a metaphor:

. . . eux aussi ont été défricheurs; non seulement défricheurs du champ spirituel qu'ils ont trouvé si inculte et rendu si fécond, mais bien aussi défricheurs du champ matériel, où nous sommes heureux de cueillir quelque adoucissement aux privations si grandes et si nombreuses dans ces contrées lointaines.[3]

This will be the dominant identification not only of his own mission memoirs, but also of most of his successors in this special form of writing. The nomads, here, are not characterized by their own distinctive nations. They are referred to as "les excellents sauvages" (p. 77 *et passim*) and other anodine phrases which contrast sharply with the sympathetic realism of Taché's other work. Links with the mother land are forged, as in the thought of tears wept at the Lakehead being washed down to the shores of the St. Lawrence. The spirit of law and order is uppermost. Mgr Taché was obviously satisfied when Father André became a military agent for the American government and pacified the Sioux Indians where the cavalry had failed to suppress them. He does not appear to object to the agricultural

[3]Alexandre-Antonin Taché, *Vingt années de missions dans le Nord-Ouest de l'Amérique*, 2nd ed. (Montreal: Cadieux & Derome, 1888), 86.

invasion of Minnesota. He makes no plea for the nomadic life which was being ousted; he regards it simply as barbaric.

The two sides of Taché's thought seek by stealth rather than open conflict to gain possession of him. The tension which might have made a great writer is absent, though there is enough tension to make him more interesting to read than most of his kind. The issue of his duality is nebulous, though it is easier to imagine him welcoming civilization with Christian resignation than with apostolic triumph.

The outside view of the North-West is represented by Mgr Laflèche, whose doctrines of national cohesion and of the missionary vocation appeared in the Three Rivers parish newspaper, and in his book, *Quelques Considérations* . . . (1866). Referring to Hebrew and other history, he explained that, like families, nations have a corporate being. Providence has a plan for each nation, which is free to desert its destiny and perish, or fulfil its divine purpose and flourish. History clearly shows that the handful of Frenchmen in North America were sent to convert the Indians to Christianity. Their descendants, he maintained, are a nation of priests, placed by God to save the whole continent.

Such sophisticated theories were not inspired by the author's contact with the buffalo hunters or canoe men of the *pays d'en haut*. They are bookish ideas, echoing René-François Rohrbacher's 29-volume *Histoire universelle de l'Eglise catholique* (Paris, 1842–1849) which had accompanied Laflèche on his mission. Yet they are also an authentic response to the appeal of the virgin lands. They are, in religious garb, like the words of John O'Sullivan, asserting the American people's "manifest destiny to overspread the continent." This view contains its own element of freedom, the freedom of a Napoleon to impose order on a continent. It is fundamentally opposed to the spontaneous freedom of the buffalo hunters.

Mgr Laflèche was not the only Napoleonic Canadian in his generation. The hero of Gérin-Lajoie's *Jean Rivard le défricheur* (1862) is a little conquering emperor whose natural ascendancy is both evident and admired. His leisure in the forest is divided between reading *The Imitation of Christ* and a history of Napoleon. His servant calls him "mon empereur."

Jean Rivard's little colony in the forest is a model of the

French-Canadian patriarchy and a microcosm of all empires. It expands and prospers under the protection of Divine Providence and the harmonious administration of its founder, who never fails to consult and agree with his friend the priest. The novel brings to life the same feelings about expansion as those of Mgr Laflèche. Expansion is a spiritual duty, rewarded with prompt material success. It is a bulwark against emigration and loss of French-Canadian identity. While *Jean Rivard* does not envisage the conversion of Indians, it does provide another way of increasing the number of the faithful, since it not only stops losses, but also advocates early marriage and the foundation of new villages.

In situating his novel in the Eastern Townships, Antoine Gérin-Lajoie opened interest in this tract of *pays d'en haut* and also hit on the literary principle of the pseudo-North. This was rough virgin land calling for a spirit of adventure, but not too far from Mother Church's apron strings. There was no question of having to adopt the life of the *coureurs de bois*. The hero is nevertheless characterized by courage, independence, closeness to nature, untutored practical skills which come forth to meet needs of all kinds, and by a subtle strength which is equal to that of the forest itself. These are all the virtues, real or legendary, of the *coureurs de bois* and *voyageurs*. They have been transferred to the pioneer, and combined with other virtues more proper to the stable life.

The rival figure of the *voyageur* has had an astounding vitality. Formed when pictures of French-Canadian life were the dominating interest in prose, this folk type is unmistakably continuous from Joseph-Charles Taché to Régine Hubert-Robert and Léo-Paul Desrosiers. Both of the two former writers refer explicitly to a collective type which they have constructed from various sources including personal contact, and there can be no doubt of Desrosiers's implicit use of the same type. By comparison, the farming type has had a meteoric history. From Antoine Gérin-Lajoie to Blanche Lamontagne (flourishing about 1920) this figure was undoubtedly more successful than the *voyageur*. Yet since 1930 his only real progress has been to become a figure of fun. Serious attempts to continue the theme of pioneering perfection are quite lamentable as literature.

Félix-Antoine Savard is the only serious exception, partly because L'Abatis is based on fact. But fact is not realism. The introduction presents the author's glowing ideas, and the memoirs which follow are rather tedious, apart from the author's own lyrical effusions on the land. He dreamed of making a new Peribonka at Abitibi, of bringing a depressed proletariat back to the natural life, of settling the semi-nomadic lumberjacks, and of placing them all in a little Christian paradise in the North:

Puis, le souvenir du champ paternel, et certaines choses que nous leur suggérions: une vie simple, libre, ordonnée, un bien qu'ils posséderaient, une maison, une femme, éveillaient en eux de bons désirs et suscitaient de généreuses énergies.

Telle fut cette fertile saison de 1935 où cinquante hommes pères de familles et jeunes gens, résolurent de nous suivre à la conquête du Nord.[4]

Joseph-Charles Taché celebrated the folk type of the voyageur and also made it a model for Christian heroes, thus making the same fusion of values as Gérin-Lajoie. His hero's life is governed by adventure and filled with knowledge of the forest, combined with obedience and fidelity, which sanctify the whole world of Forestiers et voyageurs (1863). Père Michel is an appealing character, with a sense of fun that is communicated to the reader. His wings are cut but not crippled by the author's contrivance to make him into a pious social being at peace with a well regulated hierarchy. He is the voyageur of the days of the big companies, admired for his prowess, endurance and all-round skills. His taste for independence is not developed, and he has been effectively purged of any licentiousness which may have been associated with his trade. In short, Joseph-Charles Taché made a respectable neighbour of what had been a rebel.

The comparative success of the voyageur is not due to the artistic superiority of Joseph-Charles Taché over Gérin-Lajoie. His Père Michel is just as old-fashioned as Jean Rivard. But the voyageur figure seems capable of endless renewal. The combined work of Providence and of a society which is not corrupt like its neighbours appears to produce a man especially suited to

[4]Félix-Antoine Savard, L'Abatis (version définitive) (Montreal: Fides, 1960), 16.

spreading the influence of civilization by his own activities in the *pays d'en haut.*

A chapter on lumber camp government, an idealization of the authoritarian system, shows how the harmony of law and order can be carried into the forest. Yet the author makes the piety of his bushmen seem to be natural, as well as a result of their privileged upbringing. For good measure, a Jesuit missionary of the *ancien régime* is worked into the episodic narrative, and with him his pious Montagnais converts. The presence of the *voyageur* is loosely associated with the conversion of Indians, because he is kind and understanding, and wins their friendship. The fact that he has much in common with the Indians and is accepted by them, whereas the English are not, gives the *voyageur* a share in the natural possession of the land. The implication that he is swindled by legal powers is not expressed, but Taché does state that the *voyageur* has, for two centuries, discovered and traversed all the continent. The idea is implicit that this constitutes the kind of discovery and occupation on which rights of possession are founded, and as we have noted earlier, writers like to show that through the *voyageur* the French Canadians have some sort of legal right to most of North America. It is a right based on a feeling that their occupation was natural, whereas occupation by military and economic force is not.

Taché's traditional *voyageur* is thus placed in the centre of a triad, Nature, Indians, Religion, to which he can give meaningful cohesion. In reading the varied episodes, we are constantly aware of the prior assumption that the *voyageurs* were there to spread a good influence. Providentially placed, they were also providentially endowed:

Le voyageur canadien est un homme au tempérament aventureux, propre à tout, capable d'être, tantôt, successivement ou tout à la fois, découvreur, interprète, bûcheron, colon, chasseur, pêcheur, marin, guerrier. Il possède toutes ces qualités *en puissance,* alors même qu'il n'a pas encore eu l'occasion de les exercer toutes.[5]

This impressive list of qualities, plus a few others like happiness and attractive personality, equipped him to carry out his civilizing mission.

[5]Joseph-Charles Taché, *Forestiers et voyageurs,* 2nd ed. (Montreal: Fides, 1946), 14.

This mission is made more explicit by the conclusion of *Forestiers et voyageurs* which, like a picaresque novel in form though not in moral tone, has an overall plan linking the episodes. The reason Père Michel left to become a *voyageur* is that he had injured a man. In the best *coureur de bois* tradition he was an outlaw, or rather a semi-outlaw since his victim was only an Englishman trying to enforce unjust laws. The sequence culminates in Père Michel's return home to see whether this man had been saved. Taché plays heavily on the double sense that the English officer was saved, not from death, but from heresy. His deathbed conversion was effected by the example of a kind French-Canadian mother who nursed his wounds, and fulfils the vision of the common people as part of a great missionary purpose. The venerable rogue goes to thank Sainte Anne de Beaupré, and the reader is satisfied with the mysterious power of *le rayonnement français*.

Joseph-Charles Taché clothes this idealized and symbolic figure with historical reality through the provision of ample details. He gives a solid picture of traditional *voyageur* life with exact descriptions of dress, food, pleasures such as there were, methods of building, repairing and using canoes, and above all the geographical routes which were followed, with the accumulated associations of each place name. Yet little notes of falsehood, attenuation and delicate omission suggest that the author had to force the different elements of his type together. He omits, for instance, the curious fact noted by Miss G. L. Nute, that the *voyageurs* wore loin-cloths and leather thigh-hose, rather than breeches.[6] He explains Breton and Indian words at great length, but conspicuously avoids the etymology of French-Canadianisms like *le couque, le camp* and *le flatte*. In small details like this, as in the major significance of the *voyageur* legend, Taché has had to falsify the traditional *libertin* in order to appropriate his courage, prowess and success to the theme of *rayonnement*. However broadly he wanted to interpret the notion of folk missionaries, he recognized that he could not leave the bearers of the higher civilization dressed like Montaigne's cannibals, speaking like employees of the English, and behaving like real *coureurs de bois*.

His skills, his moral significance and his picturesque appear-

[6]Grace Lee Nute, *The Voyageur* (New York: Appleton, 1931), 13–14.

ance are essential parts of Taché's *voyageur* type, bound together by the omnipresent notion of travel. Without this he could not be a *voyageur*, and without his flight from law and order into the North-West he would not be complete. Taché has transformed the classic French-Canadian journey, according to his own doctrines about the French heritage, by adding moral purpose. This he has brought close to the heart of the tradition by attaching it to the journey itself. Traditional *voyageurs*, he states, always return to their parish steeple; his own Père Michel does so with a distinct purpose in mind. Thus, the journey contains the centripetal element which is essential to the whole concept of *rayonnement*, and is associated with a Providential conversion. Despite the strains which such interpretation puts on it, the feeling of the journey *en haut* survives, in *Forestiers et voyageurs,* as something vital, adventurous and a trifle reckless.

In *Les Engagés du Grand Portage* and *Nord-Sud*, Léo-Paul Desrosiers brings the *voyageur* legend up to date by being more historically complete and true. His picture of the men who effectively occupied the North-West by their trading activities is not subordinated to the idea of the civilizing mission. The principal characters in *Les Engagés* are frank villains. The hero of *Nord-Sud* abandons the heroine because he cannot face the monotonous life of a pioneer. All of this in 1938 and 1931 was rather novel, and still makes a striking contrast with the ingenuous humbug that is the base of *rayonnement* literature. Talent and truth make this chapter of Canadian history into real historical novels, and not just a canoe-load of plaster saints.

Details of the journey are preserved, re-told with a narrative verve, and made to enter into the characterization and plot. The traditional route to the original lakehead fort at Grand Portage is followed, with enough topographical references to be traced on a map: the Ottawa and Mattawa rivers, Lake Nipissing, French River, Georgian Bay, Manitoulin Island, and so on. The portages are described with enough incident to show their dangers and hardships, together with details of weights carried and equipment used. There is in all this some of the consecrated value given by the *Song of Roland* to warlike accoutrements. The life of the *voyageur*, with his dress, sleeping arrangements and tobacco, is not omitted. The eternal *sagamité* has not changed in any basic respects since Sagard's time, though standards of hygiene must have improved, if the author is not embellishing his account of its preparation. The guides still rely on memory and experience rather than charts. Loyalty to the leader is axiomatic, despite notable lapses. The ceremonies of arrival and departure, described in colourful detail, have been cut down to size, but not omitted. In short, Léo-Paul Desrosiers has not abandoned the picture of an attractive *voyageur* possessing the continent by knowledge, tradition, and an established way of life which should command the respect of all fair-minded men. He is better informed and more discreet, but painting the same glowing picture as the lines of Louis Fréchette which present "Ces fiers coureurs des bois, / Les canots sur l'épaule et la raquette aux pieds" as heroic flag planters:

> Ce sont de fiers enfants de la nouvelle France,
> Sans songer aux périls, sans songer aux souffrances,
> Ils vont, traçant toujours leur immortel sillon,
> Au pôle, s'il le faut, planter leur pavillon.[7]

The sense of possession is not absent from that picture. Nor, in spite of care for historical truth, is the occasional exaggeration. The *engagés* are described as "des athlètes . . . recrutés avec soin dans les vieilles paroisses du Bas-Canada."[8] This improbable description is contradicted by the accounts of Miss Nute, who makes the point that the canoe itself called for men of unprepossessing stature, though hardy and agile. Desrosiers is able to maintain the impression of a superior race of men, without whom the whole North-West would have been inaccessible. He often reminds his reader of the traditional ability of the sons of the St. Lawrence, and of their ubiquity across the continent. Thus he transfers onto simple employees the great struggle for possession which took place between the rival trading companies.

The character of the French Canadian is shown as the key to possession. His kindness to the Indians, one of the reasons for this, is shown with special insistence. It is the moral justification for *rayonnement*, for the occupation which did not take place.

[7]Louis Fréchette, *La Légende d'un peuple* (Paris: Librairie illustrée, 1887), 96.

[8]Léo-Paul Desrosiers, *Les Engagés du Grand Portage* (Paris: Gallimard, 1938), 10.

Its place was usurped by the other method of possession: ruthlessness. After an initial attempt to balance good *voyageurs* with bad ones and to create a range of differences in character, the novel becomes a matter of black versus white. The conclusion is a spiritual victory to compensate for the material victory of the wicked, who are mostly, but not all, Scots. Louison Turenne, the ideal type of the French-Canadian *voyageur*, has lost his chance of advancement and riches, but his integrity remains unassailable. Those who have given in to the unscrupulous demands of the companies, on the other hand, having lost the best part of themselves, have lost all. The spiritual empire of French Canada survives in its own mysterious way, and is greater than the material empire.

Les Engagés du Grand Portage presents one more complex problem. The author has contrasted his virtuous hero with the despicable Nicolas Montour. The latter fascinates Desrosiers, who demonstrates each trick in the ascent to power without tiring. At each one, his own admiration for the villain is irrepressible. The political struggle in this novel may seem shallow but Montour's crude tactics are far from being unrealistic. With the vision of Montour's pettiness as the fatal flaw in all human organizations, Desrosiers could have been a rustic C. P. Snow, or a Machiavelli. There is no tragedy, because the author's aim is to demonstrate the victory of free will. This is what saved Turenne from corruption, cajoling, and blackmail; he stubbornly did right and refused to do wrong. Nevertheless, the really convincing picture of willpower combined with freedom is in Montour. This man fights against his own ineptitudes, against more skilful rivals and more powerful leaders, against the terrible elements of the North, and wins:

Ils luttent. Montour est indomptable. A plusieurs reprises il passe à la ronde la gourde de rhum qui réchauffe momentanément; il consulte la boussole, remet l'expédition sur sa route, surveille la tenue des hommes. Et sous la direction de sa volonté froide, les hommes vont, tremblants, le dos courbé. . . . [P. 125]

Montour lives on a kind of freedom which seems to be a faithful echo of the old *coureurs de bois*. Like his ancestors, the author will not resolve the contradictions in his own attitude to the subject, except in the concept of a higher duty.

The same could hardly be true of Alain Grandbois, whose poetical vision of the universe refuses all security. His life of Jolliet ought therefore to find some profounder sense in the explorer's obsession. However, *Né à Québec* is not the best of Grandbois. It is on the other hand very striking that he should have started his published works with material drawn from the *rayonnement* tradition, and that most of his subsequent works draw on the idea of the journey for possession of an elusive world. The literary tradition of Canada was in fact a starting point for his cosmic explorations, which have made him subsequently appear to be a most un-Canadian poet.

In fact, Grandbois's use of the adventurous journey as a poetic rather than historical theme has some antecedents in French-Canadian literature. William Chapman and Albert Ferland have both tried to capture the austere beauty of the North in verse. René Chopin's dying adventurers have no historic personality, but simply represent the part of us that responds to the indefinite appeal of the North. Grandbois's poems carried this process of abstraction further, so that it is not possible to say that his travel imagery is directly derived from the "Northern" tradition. For this reason his poems will not be discussed here. Nevertheless, the sense of adventure in his biography of Jolliet is a development of the *rayonnement* theme which shows, at least by hindsight, the way to his later works.

Né à Québec opens with a long preparatory section which establishes the historical setting for Louis Jolliet's career. God, King and Glory are present, as are many explorers and heroes of the early colonies. Present, too, are some of the colourful details that usually go with them:

Jolliet et Péré discutèrent les marchés parmi l'épaisse fumée des pipes et le choc des brocs de bière. Parfois, pour sceller un engagement, on buvait ce genièvre de feu que fournissait les bateaux hollandais. Alors les hommes devenaient bavards. Ils disaient leurs randonnées à travers les forêts interminables, la descente de rivières inconnues, la surprise des rapides, la découverte de portages. L'Aventure s'installait au cœur des récits.[9]

It is true that Grandbois is leading up to his own sense of adventure, but on the whole his material is not very different

[9]Alain Grandbois, *Né à Québec* . . . (Paris: Albert Messein, 1933), 99.

from that of Desrosiers and G. Dugas. The traditional feeling for the adventures of the national heroes, for the possession of new lands in the name of France, is coefficient with the poetic adventure, dominant, even, which is surprising in view of Grandbois's later works. The two things that are most untraditional in his treatment of history are his prose style and the deliberate absence of bigotry in showing the mosaic of fragmentary motives which led to departure and exploration. Speaking of the explorer's grandfather, he evokes the different enticements to leave France —geographical curiosity, possibility of finding precious stones, hunting and fishing, curious new tastes—and concludes: "On racontait . . . Que ne racontait-on pas? Il parlait aussi de Dieu, du Roy" (p. 10). Of the young Jolliet he says: "Il croyait en sa vocation. Il l'appelait de toute son âme. Mais s'avouait-il que son désir ne tenait qu'aux seules sollicitations d'une vie aventureuse?" (p. 73).

As in private motives, so in exterior events, Grandbois shows the French spread as a confused affair. The Jesuits are shown in their well known political intrigues against the rival orders; but no less justice is done to their courage, kindness and sincere religious purpose. Jolliet himself is shown, like all the conventional *voyageur* types, as capable of impressing and winning over the Indians. He can swim like them, paddle a canoe like them, endure like them. So his Iroquois hostage shows him a new route via Niagara Falls, a handsome gift on the lines of possession by knowledge. On the other hand, the same Iroquois has three eloquent pages to explain why he does not trust French priests any more than other white men. Jolliet himself is later able to reflect that tribes suing for French friendship see in drink and fire-arms a conspicuous advantage over their neighbours.

—Ta présence réjouit nos cœurs et flatte notre orgueil. Ton Dieu est grand, et nous l'honorons. Ton Ononthio dirige nos actes comme un vrai chef. . . .

. . . Jolliet admira la perfection de leur jeu. Il savait que chaque tribu tentait de conserver pour elle seule la faveur de l'amitié française. La rassade et les mousquets conféraient vis-à-vis des voisins une supériorité sans conteste. [P. 166]

Father Allouez, though devoted to the spread of Christianity, is not deceived as to the results: in Grandbois's narrative he comments on the fragility of the new faith and the persistence of superstitions (p. 103). Such candour is not to be found in any of the modern missionaries until about 1950, so that Grandbois's character in 1933 marks quite an important change. In fact, he seems to have started the process of putting a sense of balance into French-Canadian ancestor worship.

This is a worthy end in itself, but for Grandbois it is only a starting point. The urge for possession, stripped of all its varnish, is a complex struggle between Jesuits, Sulpicians, government, *coureurs de bois* and other individualists. Out of this only one simple truth can emerge: it is the attraction of Adventure. It is this, and not mechanical piety, that strikes Grandbois as the meaning which *rayonnement* offers the French Canadian:

A un porteur qui plaisantait sur l'existence de ce fleuve que nul témoin n'avait pu encore se vanter d'avoir vu, Marquette, en souriant, répondit par les adieux d'Isabelle-la-Catholique à Colomb: "Si la terre n'est pas Créée, Dieu la fera jaillir pour Toi du néant, afin de justifier ton audace". . . . [P. 161]

From the real, tangible historical and geographical feeling for discovery, Grandbois looks towards the abstract sense of adventure. His Jolliet is an empire builder, but his conquests are forever rising off the ground into a spiritual realm analogous to, rather than identical with, that of the missionaries and civilizers.

The most fundamental quality that Grandbois has drawn from his historical topic is the sense of vitality. This is what gives the story of French *rayonnement* a unity which transcends the plotting and counter-plotting of jealous rivals, the contradictory motives of trade, power and evangelization, the uneasy compromises between the means and the end. In his own case it was to develop into the vitality of the poetic gesture which, though it is beyond the scope of this book to assess it, probably has a considerable debt to traditional history.

The theme of vitality is present in all the best samples of *rayonnement* literature. The dual heroes of *Maria Chapdelaine* are driven by a supra-rational urge to move ever northward, one as a settler, the other as a lumberjack. This is finally converted by Maria's angel voices into the supra-rational quality of endurance. In *Sources*, Léo-Paul Desrosiers waters that endurance down to a rational medical theory. The basic premises are that we are more closely linked to the soil than we know, and that every second generation should return to the land to renew this contact. Young people living in our insipid suburban society may, by returning to the land, both recover their own strength and revitalize the country. The aim is a pact between urban and rural values, with *rayonnement* as a real force in modern conditions. The novel is consequently weaker than *Maria Chapdelaine*, but recognizably of the same inspiration.

Yves Thériault and Marius Barbeau both transfer the traditional theme of national survival from their own society to a setting which gives them artistic detachment. They are both able to see collective vitality and cultural conflicts as a moving and intricate pattern. In the choice of Indian or Eskimo societies as the centre of the struggle, these authors have made the literary tradition of survival come full circle, though without any predominantly ironic purpose.

In *Le Rêve de Kamalmouk*, Marius Barbeau shows that the struggle between tribal custom and "white" civilization can have only one outcome. This is not because the latter is intrinsically superior. Its local representatives are often crude and lacking in discernment, whereas the tribal relations of the Indians are capable of maintaining an admirable level of justice, and a refined diplomacy expressed through rituals which, though alien to us and therefore apparently barbaric, reveal considerable elegance to the penetrating anthropologist. The reason they fall before the rough justice of the "Mounties" is that they are decadent, whereas the encroaching civilization is in a phase of vigorous expansion. Through disease, a loss of conviction in rituals and superstitions, failure to enforce their own penalties rigorously, and an exaggerated awe of the white man's power, Barbeau shows the Indians' all-round decline. Unable to defend their own values or to understand the values of the encroacher, they become the tragic victims of misunderstanding. This gives rise to resentment, the most decadent of all collective attitudes.

There is nothing to suggest that *Le Rêve de Kamalmouk* is an allegory or a deliberate transposition of French-Canadian problems. It is based on Indian songs recorded by Marius Barbeau, and its chief aim is to give the reader an imaginative reconstruction of the life of the people whom the author has studied. The dramatic situation on which the novel is based it none the less a development of the well known survival and expansion themes, and draws on the French-Canadian understanding of them all the time.

Although the author's sympathies are clearly with the tribe, he creates a searching dialogue on the question of assimilation. His sympathetic hero Kamalmouk is all for progress and would like to see his people freed from the restrictions of customs, able to be individuals, like the white men he knows. The tragedy results from his vacillations and from the very imperfect understanding which exists between the different peoples. Consequently the novel's structure is essentially the conflict of two conflicts: the individual versus the tribe, and the tribe versus the foreigners.

The structure of *Agaguk* is almost identical. Less of an anthropologist, Yves Thériault has put more of his own problems of revolt and conflict into the Eskimo characters he has created. His later novel, *Cul-de-sac*, throws ample light on the conflict between Agaguk and his tribe: it is the vital revolt of youth and individuality against a rigid and restrictive society, like the revolt of Thériault's generation of French-Canadian writers against paternalism such as that of Duplessis. Agaguk differs from Kamalmouk most obviously in that he is successful. His revolt is not weak or vacillating, and is not a transfer of allegiance from one civilization to another.

On the other hand, the question of a collective struggle against a civilizing agency has not been abandoned. There is no doubt about the author's own disillusionment with the myth of *rayonnement*. Firstly, there is no sign of a powerful French spread, and the three main characters are not French. Secondly, their presence is not wholly beneficial to the Eskimos; Brown is an illicit swindler who corrupts the Eskimos with liquor; McTavish is a legalized swindler, who could help the Eskimos but has no interest in doing so; Henderson's higher values are ineffectual despite his sincerity. Thirdly, Henderson, the best agent of our civilization, is not a priest but a "Mountie"; the circumstances of his death recall in many lurid details the murder of Fathers Rouvière and Leroux at Bloody Falls,[10] so that there is reason to

[10]Cf. George Whalley, "Coppermine Martyrdom," *Queen's Quarterly*, LXVI (1959), 591–610.

suppose a fairly deliberate transfer from the traditional missionary to secular tutelage.

In spite of these very serious differences, the question of cultural penetration is still the same. The presence of trade, whether legal or not, changes life for the Eskimo. In complete freedom, he could choose good or evil from the changes offered. Cotton and whisky are two commodities shown to express this choice. However, the choice will never be made in complete freedom, because the traders are not disinterested. Under complete control, the prohibition of whisky and the application of our alien law, misunderstanding and damaging resentments would arise. Complete refusal by the Eskimos to accept any outside influence at all would result in stagnation. Thériault seems to find the answers to these problems in human vitality. Adventurous men like Agaguk, who are willing to fight the problem, can find the way to progress without loss of integrity. It is Agaguk's own vigour, not the wisdom of Henderson, that produces a higher understanding.

Thériault's is then a moralizing art. The principle he expounds through his Eskimos could apply to any other people caught between an overwhelming alien influence and an oligarchy of their own. He has looked to the traditional field of *rayonnement*, and from it brought a tonic for unhealthy doctrines of survival. Freedom, in such measure as specific societies can maintain it, is the real defence of collective values. The notion that individual submission is necessary for the sake of collective freedom is as false as it appears. Like all really vigorous moralists, Thériault opposes conventional, superficial codes of belief and conduct, to seek out something strong, simple and apparently fundamental.

Yves Thériault is aware of the value of the society, and cannot conceive of an individual without one. His Indian hero, in *Ashini*, dies as his tribe disintegrates. His outsider, in *Le Dompteur d'ours*, advises all the amorous village women to return to their husbands, and in fact helps all the maladjusted to settle down again. In *Agaguk*, tribal solidarity has a real meaning in spite of defections and corruption. Agaguk's village guards its freedom with all the collective understanding which has for centuries defended the Eskimo against a cruel nature. Liberty is conceived in a chain of ruthless forces similar to the predatory chain. A major society, because of its expansive vigour, encroaches upon a minor one, the minor one limits the freedom of the individual, yet all these forces are balanced in a constant struggle to wrest a living and some human dignity from the blind force of nature, and from each other.

Ashini is another attempt to penetrate the *rayonnement* myth to find the real meaning of freedom on the scale of conflicting cultures. It is made without the strong narrative or violent conflicts of *Agaguk*, because the Montagnais, with whom it deals, are a fallen people. In the twilight of his own culture and of his old age, the last Abenaki contemplates the problem of "white" encroachment. In this novel, Yves Thériault varies from lyrical to platitudinous, but on the whole his conclusion, with the Montagnais Messiah reversing the roles of conquered and conqueror, barbarian and civilizer, is the most original artistic use of the theme of *rayonnement*.

The novel opens with death. Ashini buries his wife with great insistence on his tribal customs, explaining those customs in detail to the reader so that they may be preserved. He generally evokes a kind of fidelity to dead things which is similar to the early literature of French-Canadian survival. In spite of the overwhelming evidence of the death of his once proud people and its way of life, he declares that he will continue:

Continuer, c'est un dessein de logique. Pour qui sait se relever et continuer, la tempête devient clémente, le froid moins mortel, le mal moins acharné, le destin plus propice. Tomber, certes, qui en est exempt! Puis se relever. Puis continuer.[11]

Already, this kind of persistence has something about it which is more than the survival theme of fidelity. The comfort which Ashini draws from the never-ending struggle rather than from providential victory probably owes as much to Albert Camus as to François-Xavier Garneau. His persistence will in fact bear no material fruit, and the novel ends in death.

The problem of racial decay in this novel resembles the bad sociology which French-Canadian critics complain of in their literature. The attempt to express the feelings of the conquered Indians is not too convincing. However, when specific references to French domination and history are made, it becomes clear

[11]Yves Thériault, *Ashini* (Montreal: Fides, 1960), 27.

that this is principally a way of developing the wider theme, and inverting standard attitudes such as those of the missionaries. Ashini notes that the defeat and humiliation of his people are partly due to the fraud by which French values have been forced upon them, and partly due to large scale desertion by the Montagnais. This is exactly the message of the older moralists of French Canada, inveighing against the Act of Union and emigration. In the matter of domination, the same law applies to all. Ashini himself has a racial prejudice against the Crees and others. Thériault has implicitly rejected the assumption of a French-Canadian duty to convert all other peoples, who are obliged to desert their own traditions. He has also rejected the intrinsic value of all such conversions, and reduced the matter to the same law as survival in nature. This is the vital struggle, and Ashini is scandalized that a superior people cannot recognize that the only higher struggle is a joint struggle of men in the face of nature. Promises of God and King are empty, if the new power cannot prove that it surpasses in some way the chain of predatory force.

A parable, supposedly from Montagnais folklore, emphasizes the point. The first wolf pack was formed when one wolf had the cunning to see that society was a method of overcoming the superior strength of a lone moose. This was a new application of the *loi du plus fort*. New discoveries were made through collective cunning that overcame the simple forms of strength. Already, some wolves were left behind: those unable to accept this innovation left the rest, and have no posterity. A second parable makes Ashini's own position more clear. An elderly wolf, wounded by a weasel, lies in hiding to recover his strength. He looks back on his success as leader of the pack, and with resentment on the young usurper. He determines to hide his weakness and continue the struggle for leadership. Wounded a second time, he howls for help, and is devoured by his rival. Ashini, like the wolves, recognizes the fatal law of survival of the strongest. Like the old wolf, he is fighting against the inevitable. His only hope is to think of another advance from the law of simple force.

It is by a last effort of intelligence and sacrifice that Ashini wins. All his remaining vitality is concentrated into a device that will overcome the law of nature, that will make him surpass human nature, and convert the defeat of the Abenaki into an everlasting victory, himself into its Messiah. As a savage, living close to the predatory force of nature, he was resigned to its common law. In the hypocrisy of the "white" administration, he is able to see something that corresponds to his Indian pride: man needs more than the law of force, he needs to save face. Ashini's solution consists simply of challenging the Christian French-Canadian power to demonstrate the higher values in the name of which it has destroyed his people.

Having issued a naive formal challenge to The Big White Chief, Ashini sacrifices himself on the sign post of the Betsiamits Indian Reserve. Upon the symbol of their victory, he has implanted himself, Christ-like, the symbol of their failure to rise above the common law and predatory rule. The higher civilization has proved unable to match his human dignity; it is meaningless, because it has not made an intelligent advance on the law of nature.

Ashini, the epilogue shows, is perpetuated in his heathen paradise "pour avoir mené . . . un combat héroïque et sans issue" (p. 169). This is the familiar device of inverting values to make material defeat into a spiritual victory, a key device of the *rayonnement* tradition. Is has been transferred from the hands of the Very Christian Monarch's successors to those of an infidel demanding that Man himself should create a higher justice. The power of overcoming the natural man has been given to an unhappy savage. At the same time, likeness to Christ has been given to the most stubborn recusant.

The Unhappy Savage is probably a new literary figure, though of course a derivative of Lahontan's device for criticizing French civilization. The Counter-Christ, even regarded only as a challenge to tepid Christians to look to their values, amounts to a powerful and bold creation. He holds himself responsible for creating a human dignity by means of an endless struggle against superior but unconscious forces. It is a meaningful advance on the spiritual empire, a French-Canadian device *par excellence*. Yves Thériault, despite a streak of sentimentality towards the hero, an unconvincing realism and some amateur philology, has a creative vitality which is the artistic equal of his subject. He is the writer who has really made something of this topic.

Although he has apparently turned the meaning of *rayonne-ment* upside down, Thériault has remained faithful to the real core of the movement. His works are essentially an appeal to vigour. It is for this reason that a number of the most hackneyed devices take on new shapes and meanings with him. Whereas so many pious biographers are like idolaters before the created image of the explorer or pioneer, Thériault, like Alfred Des-Rochers, has made the active principle of these traditional heroes into an artistic principle.

Vigour is, with him, an artistic principle, but it is also and most essentially a moral principle. The whole being of the *rayon-nement* theme is vested in the expanding community; it is a social matter, and therefore matter for a moralist. Most of the works devoted to it fail as literature, not because they are too involved with the moral question, but because they make it too superficial. Thériault attacks his problem vigorously, seeking the essential and not merely the local application. His moralizing does not eclipse his art, but is a vital part of it. Together, they have the strong, brutal simplicity which is characteristic of reforming zeal, though marred occasionally by too obvious "literary" flights.

In general, the *rayonnement* theme has been more productive of quantity than of quality in literature. The individual journey is a more successful literary form. A long tradition of hypocrisy and misrepresentation has made spiritual empires unattractive to refined writers. Even in ironic rejection it is a little disappoint-ing, mainly because the target is too easy. Only a very vigorous moralist can strip it down to what it is really worth.

On the other hand, it has been the powerful myth which has kept alive the conscious development of a written tradition on the *pays d'en haut*. From this myth the other themes related to journeys draw some of their strength, and it has kept them alive as real imaginative material over the changing periods of Cana-dian history. Its popularity establishes a link not only between present and past, but also between writer and public. It is an important factor in the common fund of French-Canadian awareness, just as the "Frontier" has been to Americans. It has kept alive, despite the choking layers of ossified idealism, because its essential quality is vitality. A persistent belief in French-Canadian life has remained at the heart of it.

The historical development of this common awareness offers an interesting view of the authoritarian spirit in French Canada. It could also throw light on the popular feeling which supports the present separatist movement. In literary creation, its worst limitation has barely been overcome. Freed by military conquest from the need to be realistic, the frustrated urge to expand produced an inflated ideal. Rhetoric is almost inescapable for the French Canadian writing on this topic, and the shadow of the unbuilt empire is everywhere. False identifications have been honoured long enough to become realities. Even the impeccable Grandbois fumbled with his adventure of Jolliet, and could only redeem himself with a book on the travels of Marco Polo. Marius Barbeau must be credited with the invention of the double conflict. This device, in a transposed setting, released the real drama of *rayonnement*, which is not French versus English in a static world, but individual versus society in a world which may be hostile to both. Yves Thériault, because of his own vitality and his very full grasp of the popular feeling, has developed that drama into the permanently unresolved conflict between human and natural values.

The complex relationship of civilized human values with nature, human or external, always involves the principle of vitality. It is the simple grasp of this principle that distinguishes Yves Thériault and enables him to plane, at times too easily, over the Gordian knots of his topics. Of these the chief is the concept of human nature. Its development in the *coureur de bois* type will be discussed in another chapter.

CHAPTER FOUR

Quest

In a general way all the works referred to above constitute a journey which could be regarded as a national saga. Antiquarian detail such as the *voyageurs*'s canoe routes may often obscure deeper significance. Yet in a number of works there is a repeated plan, in which the form of a journey is consubstantial with the writer's or created character's state of mind. In all the examples to be examined in this chapter, there is some identification of the journey *en haut* with an intense searching feeling.

The general significance of travel in various myths has to be considered as well as the more or less conscious attitudes of French travellers to New France in the seventeenth and early eighteenth centuries. Some of these, like Lescarbot in Acadia, found that Frenchmen were transformed by their new surroundings into almost perfect idyllic beings. Others, culminating in Lahontan, placed their picture of human perfection in the savage. In either case, they were engaged in a search for a new man. A few remarks from J. E. Cirlot's article on the journey in ancient symbolic traditions show that search itself is the primary sense of travel in most mythologies:

The journey is never merely a passage through space, but rather an expression of the urgent desire for discovery and change. . . . Hence, to study, to inquire, to seek or to live with intensity through new and profound experiences are all modes of travelling. . . . Primarily, to travel is to seek.[1]

Cirlot also notes other principles which will have some application in this discussion, but the urgent search was uppermost in the minds of the original travellers.

[1] J. E. Cirlot, *A Dictionary of Symbols*, trans. Jack Sage (London: Routledge & Kegan Paul, 1962), *s.v.* "Journey."

For most writers, *the* journey has been the inland one. The ocean journey has surprisingly little wonder.[2] The real voyage of discovery is the one that leads from France's foothold into the hinterland of the continent. The New World has already aged a little at the edges, but man's persistent belief in something new to be found a little further upstream has not.

This outlook corresponds to the prevailing feeling in France during the period of establishing Canada. The generous optimism of the Renaissance travellers had subsided, but through the more constrained channels of the Counter-Reformation old ideas were finding new expression, new material, new life. A kind of man who was firmly convinced of the limits of human nature was placed within reach of a new voyage of discovery, which might take him beyond those limits. The Great Adventure was over, the devious one remained.

It was obvious to all informed arrivals in Canada that the savage, Huron, Iroquois or any other, must be the man of nature about whom they had vaguely heard. As such he was a realized specimen of the hypothetical natural man, neither regenerated by Christian knowledge nor corrupted by civilized usage. Certain characteristics common to most Indians confirmed this supposition. The savage was free; that is to say that he did not conform to European laws or authority. He lived close to external nature, in that his food and clothing were rudimentary. If he ever desired anything other than what external nature supplied immediately, this was taken to be a sign of European corruption. He was resigned to his condition; for instance, he accepted death in warfare with much better grace than Europeans. These observations were enough to override any contrary evidence. The illusion was in control, and arranged or interpreted the evidence by the only system it knew. Even making due allowance for conscious motives, we may deduce from the early reports on Canadian Indians that French observers were swayed by the image of the happy savage without always realizing it.

This is particularly true of Gabriel Sagard, whose *Grand*

[2]Alain Grandbois's interest in travel themes and imagery goes far beyond his biography of Jolliet, and the sea is particularly evident in his poems. There is not enough wider evidence to establish a meaningful link between sea journeys and the *pays d'en haut*, although it undoubtedly exists in the individual case of Grandbois.

Voyage au pays des Hurons is in many senses a Canadian arche-
type. It is the first full account of the inland journey so often
related by provincial folklorists of the modern period. Like most
of the missionaries, Sagard was writing to some extent to gain
support for his own Order. Nevertheless, the reader feels fairly
satisfied that these are candid first impressions. Later, as their
conflict with the Jesuits reached what was for the Franciscans
its tragic conclusion, he wrote an enlarged account called *Histoire
du Canada*. The political bias added to the second version testi-
fies to the purity of the first. We also know from internal evidence
that Sagard lost most of his notes, so that the first published
account of contact with the Hurons is indeed what it seems, an
attempt to recollect and record the author's personal impressions
of a recently completed journey. The Jesuits, with their superior
discipline and organization, felt they were in Canada to stay, and
sent home more lengthy, leisurely accounts. Their *Relations* are
much better calculated to please potential patrons, more orderly,
more optimistic, more inclined to accommodate new information
with known truths and doctrines. It is probably for these reasons
that they are less interesting than Sagard's memoirs as an example
of the moral confusion in which Counter-Reformation man found
himself, once removed from the familiar map of human nature.

Sagard's discovery of himself and of the Hurons appears as
one experience. From the simple Recollect brother setting out
with nothing but the proper motives and a few memories of the
classics, he becomes a man with hopes, doubts and fears and a
presence which the reader just begins to share with the missionary's curious friends. In the relation of this adventure, the
only discernible form is the form of the journey itself. Neither
treatment by simple sequence in time nor treatment by simple
topics is consistent, whereas the sense of the journey beneath
these meanderings is a unifying principle with a meaningful
pattern. Sagard stumbled upon the use of the journey as an
artistic form. A hundred years later, the revival of this *genre* had
been completed, and writers of genius were using it in France,
either for utopian or for satirical effect, the latter being the
obverse of the ideal journey.

Sagard was unable to find any other sort of order because of an
unresolved inner conflict. This was due to his grave reservations

about promoting the rapid spread of French civilization. He questioned both the civilizing process and the type of society it envisaged. The *Grand Voyage* mixes this question with the religious dispute on whether man in his natural state is uncorrupted virtue or utter darkness. "Ce que la simple Nature leur enseigne," Sagard observed, was all that the Hurons knew of politeness.[3] They belched, lied, were vengeful and filthy with their food. Yet his memoirs also show a more advantageous list of qualities, evidently due to the same teacher.

These pages give the impression that praise was getting the better of Sagard, and he hastened to correct the picture. Another place shows him specifically denying "la pureté d'une nature espurée" (p. 308; M 81). He was aware of the common myth of the virtuous man of nature, aware of his own tendency to subscribe to it, and aware of a need to refute it in the name of the religion he was disseminating; "tout homme y est sujet [à l'imperfection] et à plus forte raison celuy qui est privé de la cognoissance d'vn Dieu et de la lumiere de la foy" (p. 343; M 186).

In spite of such reasonable modification, which appears in only two places, Sagard was not able to discard the idea of the good savage. The missionary was attached to his Hurons, had practical reasons for showing them in a good light, and was fascinated by the illusion of newness in a New World. He was also guided by a little ill-digested reading of the classics, which confirmed his vision of natural virtues. But above all he was guided by a prevailing image of the savage which was to emerge a century later in its most celebrated form.

A modern anthropologist would probably conclude that what impressed Frenchmen in the Indian was the affective-cognitive-instrumental unity of primitive activities. But Sagard had to describe this in the system of vices and virtues he knew. The virtues he saw in his Hurons, as he began to understand them, include piety, charity, fidelity to such moral laws as they had, military courage, asceticism and physical health. They lacked chastity. Even here, Sagard was loath to leave their deficiency unqualified. One attenuation is that they have other conjugal

[3]Gabriel Sagard, *Le Grand Voyage au pays des Hurons*, 3rd ed. (Toronto: The Champlain Society, 1939), 343; 0.186.

virtues in good measure; another is that, though promiscuous, they are not lascivious. But the best defence of Nature's ability to teach virtue is the use of hearsay evidence, which has the last word over what was actually observed. Some other Indian nations, Sagard informed his readers, were much stricter than Europeans about chastity and punished offenders by cutting off their noses.

It seems strange that having recognized important differences between one nation of Indian and another, anyone would still think of these men as direct products of a uniform nature. In this respect, Sagard may be contrasted with Samuel Hearne, a man who valued his life and saw that it depended on choosing guides for his very hazardous enterprise. He clearly recognized that there were important differences between what he called Northern and Southern Indians, who had distinct moral traditions of their own. Furthermore, he was able to distinguish individual characters among the Indians he knew, and assess them in terms of universal types of failing.

Hearne was able to see that the tribal man's fear of ridicule amounted to a very rigid limitation of individual freedom, whereas Sagard was not. What he and his readers (including Jean-Jacques Rousseau) thought they saw was not so much a society as an assembly of free men and women. Freedom appeared to be the real difference between civilized persons and men of nature. Unable to recognize alien forms of social restriction for what they were, most observers assumed that savages had none. All of this led up to the concept of a society not based on central authority. Sagard actually used the word *République* and described a society which was a prototype for Montesquieu and Voltaire. Chiefs were generally elders who led their people by exhortation and example. Their position could be inherited only if the incumbent were also heir to the virtue of his forefathers. Otherwise, tribes returned to the elective system on which their kingdoms were originally founded. There is some detail on the use of assemblies as an organ of government (pp. 346–47; M 196–200). All in all, Sagard was describing the opposite of the absolute authority that Richelieu was imposing on France, and which was to be projected onto Canada in an even more extreme form. The *pays d'en haut* were already a symbol of liberty.

The most striking feature of the travel sequence in Sagard's *Grand Voyage* is the contrast between the going and the return. On the sea voyage from France to Quebec there are two chapters (if we include the first, which declares the author's intentions in setting out). A short chapter describes the arrival in Quebec, and first impressions of Indians, traders, and mission houses. The fourth chapter is devoted to the main part of the journey up to the freshwater sea, and the fifth continues that journey, up to the arrival at the first Huron village. These two chapters also contain descriptions of customs, mostly relevant to the journey. The whole of the return journey is in one chapter, of which the last paragraph is the only account of the ocean crossing. This structure denotes a slow climb, with phases of joy, hardship, expectation, and loss, followed by a rapid descent, even something of a fall.

It is in the form of the *Grand Voyage* that the resolution of Sagard's dilemma is to be found. Thus, the journey itself is far more than an itinerary, it is the key to the author's deepest feelings. His obvious disappointment at being recalled to France leads directly into the sketchy conclusion. It is, without the dreams of a Coleridge, as if the writer has been interrupted by a person from Porlock. Until this point there has been no obvious elevation, and yet suddenly it is as if Sagard has been snatched away from his cloud, to be put down in the world of unpalatable necessities. It must have been evident that the Recollects had lost this mission to the Jesuits. With half-hearted promises to return he took leave of the savage companions he was just beginning to understand, and sailed for France. This last episode meant so little to him that it is merely sketched in outline, in spite of the fact that it contained adventures every bit as exciting as those of the westward journey.

Between the upward journey and the downward one Sagard had come to understand the Hurons. The upward journey explains important details (Chs. 4 and 5). The canoes were of a certain size, the camps made in certain places, and built in such and such a fashion. There is a description of the eternal *sagamité* which was to be the staple diet of the *voyageurs* for two centuries, but which the good brother could not eat at all until he had gone hungry for several days. Other hardships which he endured for the love of God include swarms of mosquitoes, hard portages, and the loneliness of being unable to speak the language of his fellows. At the same time he was able to marvel at the skill of his Indian companions in finding food on the way, at their patience with himself, and at the genius of Providence which had placed fish so plentifully in the streams. He also made his first observations on the appearance and customs of the Indians with whom he travelled and those whom they encountered. These are mostly details of face painting, hair styles, and strange manners. On the return journey these details are not repeated. They have been replaced by a more complete account of the events, in which the missionary's companions seem more like human individuals. Clearly, the author has come to know them. With this knowledge has come the ability to penetrate their motives and fears in various situations; even in their limitations, they were just men. Gone for ever is the wonder of the upward journey.

The man who has replaced it is the imperfect being known to the Counter-Reformation world. He cheats or is cheated, lies or is credulous, has moments of generosity and moments of avarice. Yet that is not all. In the impression left by the shape of Sagard's journey there emerges something more than the record of known human limits. This is not a Romantic elation in Nature. There is a feeling of achievement, as if the author had travelled up to some higher plane of understanding, penetrated some mystery, and found something like a new man, despite inconsistencies in what he actually says.

Sagard's journey was a sober challenge to accepted ideas, a re-opening of questions which had been closed either by authoritarianism or by pyrrhonism. Even if it brought no new conclusions, there was a new sense of earnest searching. The physical details of the journey anticipate nearly all those that were to become traditional. This fact reinforces the link, to be found again in later writers, between the *pays d'en haut* and the attempt to gain a new understanding of man, by seeing him, as it were, from outside.

The *pays d'en haut* continued to exercise various kinds of fascination throughout the period of French administration. Even as early as Sagard himself, there were Frenchmen such as Etienne

Brûlé who were assimilated to the life of the forest and its Indian denizens. Even on the most conformist and unsearching of minds the journey exerted its influence, for these were able to see in it the virtues of their choice. Favoured by official and general hypocrisy as well as by genuine confusion of motive and interpretation, the idea of the journey continued to be admirable and exciting. It was still a living tradition for writers of the nineteenth century. They felt obliged to obscure it beneath shallow moralizing and local colour, but the concrete symbol of the journey remained alive in the nascent literature of French Canada.

In the literary schools of the nineteenth and early twentieth centuries the journey was less admired than the farm, which represented the official side of order and stability. There was little in writing before 1930 to suggest the sudden reversal of this preference; it is explained mainly as a reaction. Nor was there much to suggest the re-emergence of the deeper sense of the journey. A few poems in which the *pays d'en haut* are conspicuously not linked to any moralizing or national purpose have already been mentioned. It is as well to remember that such liberties, such elevated Epicureanism, were condemned by Camille Roy, the literary pontiff of the time, on the grounds that exultation in the senses is pagan. There are, besides, a few writers who responded to the freedom associated with the *pays d'en haut*. James Prendergast, like Fathers Taché and Dugas, recognized that this was a more stirring connotation than *rayonnement*. His poem "Tempête" (1882) apostrophizes the wind with an appeal for its disorderly ecstasy:

> Fais tomber dans mon cœur tes torrents, ton écume,
> Et dis-moi, peux-tu le remplir?[4]

Such appearances testify to the continuing presence of the restless northward feeling, but were too rare to constitute a rebel camp. The literary possibilities of such themes were not likely to be exploited in a period of spiritual conformity. Prendergast himself obviously vacillated before his Dionysiac question.

The precise point at which the spiritual sense of the journey emerges is at the decay of the orderly superstructure which

[4]*Anthologie des poètes canadiens*, edited by Jules Fournier (Montreal: Granger frères, 1920), 119.

nationalist writers and critics had built upon French-Canadian themes. It was a decay not unlike the end of Louis XIV's France when the spirit of orthodoxy seemed to be triumphant but had exhausted itself.

The poet of the moment was Alfred DesRochers. He was the first writer to recognize clearly that the vigorous forest hero was a thing of the past. Accordingly, he is a decadent poet using traditional material. *L'Offrande aux Vierges folles* (1928) contains less folk material and more recognizable decadence than his later *A l'Ombre de l'Orford*.[5] "Mon cœur" rejects confidence in the human faculties, personifies despair with an almost physical presence, and ends with the poet's heart still unable to forget the habit of hope, which appears in the form of an imagined journey. The allusion in this case is classical, not Canadian, but is taken as representative of all journeys involving hope and despair.

> Mon cœur est un aïeul de quatre-vingt-dix ans
> Dont sont défunts les fils et dont l'épouse est morte;
> Il médite, accroupi sur le seuil de sa porte,
> Combien l'esprit est faible et sont menteurs les sens.
>
> Il dit l'inanité de l'espoir aux passants:
> Ce qu'offre le présent, l'avenir le remporte;
> Sa masure branlante où loge le cloporte
> Est la somme d'efforts et de travaux puissants.
>
> Mais il va chaque jour errer le long des grèves
> Et scrutant le lointain, hanté d'anciens rêves,
> Il met souvent sa main au-dessus de ses yeux,
>
> Pour voir si, revenant d'aventures lointaines,
> Ne songent, à l'avant de vaisseaux glorieux,
> Ses fils debout, chamarrés d'or et capitaines.

The journey in this case recalls the return of Theseus or Jason, but is general enough to contain the hopes of all discoverers.

"Atavisme" throws more light on the type of journey present in this poet's imagination, still without any Canadian allusion. His heart is now in a conquering mood, like the barbarian kings

---

[5]The second edition of *A l'Ombre de l'Orford* (Montreal: Action canadienne-française, 1930) contains an extensive selection from *L'Offrande aux Vierges Folles*. All references to DesRochers's works will be made to this edition except where otherwise indicated.

falling on a decadent empire. He dreams only of the next journey of conquest, his grief is only caused by his inability to seize the whole world at once. This is the kind of vigour, exempt from civilized refinements, which the poet of "Mon cœur" knows will never return.

> J'écoute en moi rêver l'âme d'un roi barbare
> Qui, riche de butin, mais une larme au cil,
> Regarde ses vaincus s'en aller vers l'exil,
> Avec femmes et fils, à bord d'une gabarre.
>
> Mais le chagrin tardif qui de son cœur s'empare,
> Ce n'est pas d'exposer ces êtres au péril:
> De celles qui s'en vont peut-être en était-il
> Dont il aurait aimé la pudeur qui s'effare.
>
> La reine, près de lui, branle ses diamants,
> S'évente d'une main distraite, et, par moments,
> Parle à mi-voix, soupire et gonfle ses narines;
>
> Mais le roi n'entend pas ce que la reine dit
> Et darde son œil fauve au-dessus des collines,
> Où scintillent des toits de marbres, au midi.

"Désespérance romantique" is a fully developed imaginary journey containing a certain amount of immediate allusion to the special sense of the journey in French Canada, particularly through the ancestors. "La Naissance de la Chanson" is a sequence of pictures intensely bound to their regional content, but together forming a complete journey. Other poems, including the "Fils déchu" and the "Hymne au vent du Nord" contain important journey elements. All these can be related to the Baudelairean sense of the journey, though in some cases it is clear that DesRochers has cultivated the symbol for itself, and the significance tends to be lost under decorative details. Consequently, this unusual hermetic system is easily confused with *terroir* regionalism.

Although he was acquainted with the life of the lumber camp, DesRochers was not a lumberjack, still less a *voyageur*. His main knowledge of the journey is due to the ancestral awareness of which he speaks in "Je suis un fils déchu" and elsewhere:

> Je rêve d'aller comme allaient les ancêtres;
> J'entends pleurer en moi les grands espaces blancs.

"Désespérance romantique" is the most purely imaginative journey, and is also the poem in which the whole theme is made to correspond to the shape of a journey. The journey is the real form of the poem. It opens with disgust, which is attached to static imagery, and restlessness, which finds visions distinctly related to the traditional journey to the *pays d'en haut.*

> Je partirai, furtif, dès le petit matin,
> A l'heure où le soleil rôde encore incertain,
> Derrière l'amas bleu des lointaines collines
> Que la brume revêt de blanches mousselines;
> Je partirai, furtif, et le regard tendu
> Vers quelque bourg du nord, à l'horizon, perdu
> Parmi de hauts sommets dont on ne voit les cimes
>
> . . . .
>
> Je ne veux pas revoir cette branche de lierre
> Qui s'enroule à l'entour du vieux siège de pierre,
> Auprès de la tonnelle, au milieu du jardin;
>
> . . . .
>
> Je m'en irai d'un pas effaré, dans la rue
> Dont la longueur sera par le silence accru;
> Mais quand ma marche aura dépassé les remparts,
> Je secouerai mes pieds enivrés des départs, . . .

Yearning to set out, the poet is held back both by the ramparts, which represent the dogma of civilized values and consequently a rational awareness of human failure, and by the security denoted by the maternal garden and the arbour.[6] This connotation is supported by a liberal sprinkling of abstract nouns in a denunciation of hope, friendship and love. The booming rhetoric of these words is discarded as the journey gets under way.

After this mood of exploratory restlessness, about one third of the poem, the will asserts itself and there is a feeling of upward movement. The poet will escape, like St. John of the Cross, but his mystical union will be with the strength and purity of the mountains. The escape is matched by various expressions of discomfort, because the journey is an arduous search.

> Au soleil j'offrirai ma jeunesse et ma force,
> Et les muscles puissants et souple de ma chair,
> Pour que son poids, croulant sur moi d'un zénith clair,
>
> . . .
>
> Alourdisse mon corps . . .

---

[6]Cf. Cirlot, *A Dictionary of Symbols,* "City," "Landscape."

Ce que je veux subir, c'est une douleur neuve:
Je veux savoir les maux physiques, et l'effroi
De voir les chiens rageurs aboyer contre moi;
Je veux connaître enfin la fatigue des membres,

. . . .

Je veux vivre la vie âpre des DesRochers,
L'existence remplie et dure des ancêtres,
Qui tout le jour ployés à leurs travaux champêtres,
S'endormaient, quand venait l'obscurité, si las
Que la foudre éclatant ne les éveillait pas!

The new pain is like an initiation to the new man, despite the fact that it is found partly in the image of the past. The search is for regeneration, which is echoed by the sun and moon imagery, culminating in the rise of the moon at the same time as the poet's complete purification.

The upward movement can be followed consistently through the poem, with moments of relief provided by small relapses. The profile of the journey is that of a rugged ascent. The pitch is varied by the introduction of human malice, observed by the traveller in the middle of his day, but followed by a new attempt to rise above it; by repeated references to fatigue and a rallying of the last energy; and by the last urge to overcome the mountain within the last minutes of daylight. The very end contains both an upward and a downward movement, as the poet sinks into a brutish slumber, with one moment to be aware of the moonlight filling him in place of the hope and memory which he sought to escape at the beginning.

Toute ma force éparse encore inépuisée,
Je courberai plus bas mon échine lassée
Et j'escaladerai la montagne, où surgit,
Sur le dernier fond d'or du couchant aminci,
Le bourg que je visais en partant de la ville,
Dégoûté des humains et de leur clameur vile.

Et je m'écroulerai dans la fougère, alors.
Mais avant qu'un sommeil aussi lourd que mon corps
Abolisse la gloire âpre du paysage,
Couché sur le flanc droit, du foin sur le visage,
Sans m'apercevoir même en mon néant qu'il soit
Des branches de bois morts et des cailloux sous moi,

Encore conscient, j'aurai cette minute
Unique de sentir en mon âme de brute
S'infiltrer, remplaçant la mémoire et l'espoir,
La blancheur de la lune, et le calme du soir.

Although most evidently a spiritual climb, "Désesperance romantique" contains enough local substance to be unmistakeably by the same hand as the "fils déchu" poem. In this the poet's fallen state is thrown into contrast with the vigour of his pioneer ancestors, the imagery related to historical journeys. A similar feeling of gradual climbing is present, although it leads to a fall. There is an increased richness of pictorial expression, without any great loss of significance. Once his system has been penetrated the attitude of fallen man within the decadent lumberjack is perfectly lucid. The increased brittleness of the symbols goes with the increased feeling of fragility and despair.

Je suis un fils déchu de race surhumaine,
Race de violents, de forts, de hasardeux,
Et j'ai le mal du pays neuf, que je tiens d'eux,
Quand viennent les jours gris que septembre ramène.

Tout le passé brutal de ces coureurs des bois:
Chasseurs, trappeurs, scieurs de long, flotteurs de cages,
Marchands aventuriers ou travailleurs à gages,
M'ordonne d'émigrer par en haut pour cinq mois.

Et je rêve d'aller comme allaient les ancêtres;
J'entends pleurer en moi les grands espaces blancs
Qu'ils parcouraient, nimbés de souffles d'ouragans,
Et j'abhorre comme eux la contrainte des maîtres.

"Je suis un fils déchu," like "Désespérance romantique," starts with horizontal observation, leading into a vague upward nostalgia. This takes on the precise form of an atavistic memory, which leads into an imaginary journey up to the *pays d'en haut*. The rugged ascent is marked by upward and downward movements of joy and pain. Through the real effort of carrying his imaginary burden, the poet reaches a serene realization, a high point from which he can look around on his instinctive need for adventures which will make him come to grips with nature. Then he plunges back into his fallen state, to realize that these aspirations, though real, are dead within him. From this low point, he is able once to see an upward possibility. He has trailed down some memories like Wordsworth's clouds of glory from his *coureur de bois* ancestor.

> Si d'eux qui n'ont jamais connu le désespoir,
> Qui sont morts en rêvant d'asservir la nature,
> Je tiens ce maladif instinct de l'aventure
> Dont je suis quelquefois tout envoûté, le soir;
>
> Par nos ans sans vigueur je suis comme le hêtre
> Dont la sève a tari sans qu'il soit dépouillé,
> Et c'est de désirs morts que je suis enfeuillé,
> Quand je rêve d'aller comme allait mon ancêtre;
>
> Mais les mots indistincts que profère ma voix
> Sont encore: un rosier, une source, un branchage,
> Un chêne, un rossignol parmi le clair feuillage,
> Et comme au temps de mon aïeul, coureur des bois,
>
> Ma joie ou ma douleur chantent le paysage.

One aspect of this polyvalent journey which should not be overlooked is the historical situation of Alfred DesRochers as the fallen French-Canadian man of the early twentieth century. This poet, more than any other, because unconsciously, sings the failure of the nationalist movement. The effort of writers like Lionel Groulx (though Groulx himself denied it) was to relive in Canada the glories of the past. These are those dead desires, like the leaves on a sapless tree, which DesRochers knew. His use of folk illustration is not just a superficial local colouring, not just the adoration of provincial types and symbols. It is integral to the poet's vision and also has its own depth as a traditional way of seeing things. His nostalgia, out of context, might be taken as a variant on the ancestor worship of writers like Groulx, who idealize pioneers in substantially the same way as Marie-Antoinette idealized shepherdesses.

In its context, which always shows it clearly as desires for the unattainable, it amounts to a much more serious kind of nostalgia. DesRochers is not constructing a patriotic superman, he is using the known image of the hardy ancestor to express a feeling quite unlike nationalist history. Significantly, he has revived the *coureur de bois*; the nationalists tended to avoid this semi-outlaw because it was incompatible with the paragon of virtues they needed to see in the ancestor. DesRochers's ancestor figure, a composite of *coureur de bois, voyageur,* lumberjack and pioneer, is a super-human mixture of vigour and brutality, cursing and singing his way across the continent, struggling with nature as if he were equal to it. The poet, in his decadence, does not expect to become such a superman in any literal sense, and in life he never did become a lumberjack. It is only as a poet that he rises above himself and human weakness.

It is the struggle with nature and against it that gives meaning to DesRochers's pictorial descriptions of pioneer farmers and lumberjacks. Even when portrayed with regionalist realism, they are still in this sense men of nature, and this is what they have in common with each other. Whether it is lumberjacks felling a pine or pioneer neighbours raising a barn frame, the feeling of restless triumph is the same:

> De temps en temps un coup de foudre emplit l'espace.
> C'est un pin qui s'abat devant l'homme rapace.
>
> ("L'Abattage")

> La charpente a l'aspect d'un squelette géant
> Que la mort décharna sans qu'elle ait pu l'abattre;

> Car, andouiller moisi qui brave encor l'affront,
> Pointé vers l'ennemi qu'il faut toujours combattre,
> Un sapin se dessèche au sommet d'un chevron.
>
> ("La Corvée")

Without other evidence it would be easy to think of the sonnet cycles as mere descriptive regionalism, in which the pioneer and the lumberjack find their common identity in being traditional French-Canadian heroes of the soil. But these men are both of the soil and against it, whilst the poet's own nostalgia for their brutal force is exactly like that found in his picture of the barbarian king. His "Hymne au Vent du Nord" also invokes both the ancestors and the elements in one unified nostalgia:

> Car mes aïeux, au cours de luttes séculaires,
> Subirent tant de fois les coups de tes lanières
> Que ta rage puissante en pénétra leurs sens.

In "Lorsque je pense à vous . . . " (published for the first time in *Ecrits du Canada français VII*, in 1961) the vision of savage, external nature is identified with the memory of personal love.

Nature, in all of these poems, evokes the awareness of a lost virtue, brutal but vital, and comparable with the awe with which Sagard and his contemporaries regarded the filthy brutes they called Hurons.

The journeys undertaken in both "Désespérance romantique" and the "fils déchu" poem are journeys to the *pays d'en haut*, and culminate in the same nostalgia as these portrayals of *pays d'en haut* life. The journey and the folk types are all one in the poetry of Alfred DesRochers, and it is for this reason that he has succeeded better than any other French-Canadian poet in making folk material into real poetry. Even in the descriptive sonnets, there is a distinct feeling of travel, and the lumberjack cycle is, as a sequence, a very obvious journey from a bar up to a lumber camp and back again. Through the hard, durable pictures of French-Canadian backwoods life the reader sees the dream of the "fils déchu" who made the journey only in inherited memories.

The sense of the journey as a vital illusion is present again in Gabrielle Roy's character, Alexandre Chenevert. She, even more than Alfred DesRochers, is aware of the illusory nature of the journey, and has made a hero quite incapable of living in a lumber camp. The created character, on the other hand, is not able to distinguish between the illusory and the real elements of his journey. He does at times dream of changing his occupation, but his life is determined like the routes of the Montreal tramways which are his daily journey. The gap between journeys such as his bus trip to Saint-Donat, and the spiritual adventure which Alexandre finds in them, points to the gap between man's ideal and his human situation.

The profile of Alexandre Chenevert's trip is similar to that of DesRochers's "Désespérance romantique." A prelude of horizontal searching leads into a sudden upward movement, followed by a relieved ascent to a peak of goodness. But this episode is not a poem, it is part of a novel. After the peak and a brief plateau there is a rapid fall back to the ordinary plane of existence, on which the hero will live out the rest of his life. The descent is readily comparable with that of the "fils déchu" poem and, when due allowance has been made for the differences of historical period, with that of Brother Sagard's return to Quebec and the inexorable sameness of the world he had left. As in Sagard's *Grand Voyage*, there is a feeling of a protracted and ambiguous discovery in the middle of the journey, expressed through a sojourn more or less in one place.

The prelude of reluctance before this journey shows Alexandre walking in the city streets, trying to make up his mind. He is to leave in search of happiness, and is sceptical. He is a prose Alfred DesRochers, held back by the same lack of faith in his ability to meet the challenge of his mission, and by the same reluctance to leave the ordered world in which he has lost faith. Uplifted by the hope of a happiness which will be unselfish, by a desire to believe in natural, healthy happiness, by a belief in progress, Alexandre is immediately dejected by the sight of a policeman directing the traffic. He is reminded of the opposition between order and freedom, duty and happiness. Through the immediate vision of the traffic, he feels that the individual journey is incompatible with society.

—Partez, Monsieur Chenevert, dit [le docteur.] Allez-vous-en. Débarrassez-vous. Faites une fois au moins dans votre vie ce que vous avez toujours voulu faire.

. . . .

Tel un remède, le bonheur, c'est vrai, était moins égoïste, moins déraisonnable. Il réfléchissait.—Ça a du bon sens.

. . . .

Il s'aperçut que c'était l'été, presque la fin de l'été. Mais l'été n'est-il pas plus précieux en ces derniers jours menacés? Et le bonheur, à cinquante-deux ans, plus nécessaire qu'à vingt ans?

. . . .

En honnête homme il essaya de se dire qu'il n'avait pas plus le droit d'agir à sa guise que, par exemple, le pauvre policeman planté sur le macadam, en plein soleil furieux, et faisant là-bas des gestes si fréquents que le spectacle commençait à fatiguer M. Chenevert. Alors, comme il aurait pu le faire toute sa vie au fond, il regarda ailleurs. Peut-être ne devrait-on pas répéter aux gens qu'ils ont le droit d'être heureux. La permission pourrait mener un jour à une curieuse confusion: plus d'agents aux coins des rues; plus de mineurs sous terre, plus de fileurs, plus de tisserands à leur ouvrage insalubre.[7]

All of the symbols based on travelling occur in the most naturalistic manner, which is the fine quality of Gabrielle Roy's writing.

[7]Gabrielle Roy, *Alexandre Chenevert* (Montreal: Beauchemin, 1954), 174–77.

Yet it is only in them as symbols that the meanings can be brought together. Alexandre's labyrinth of responsibilities and needs, of virtues and weaknesses can only partly be made clear by his rational argument. Its unity is to be seen in the apparently incidental descriptions. At the end of this chapter, the hero overcomes his habitual prudence, and trots through the traffic to buy a newspaper. The journey has begun because Alexandre has made the discovery that man desires happiness.

However prosaic the naturalistic description of the bus journey is, the inescapable poetic feeling for departure is also present, as well as the deeper significance of the search. Alexandre leaves early in the morning, secretly. Of course, living in an apartment building, he is not unobserved. His fragile aspiration to escape like St. John of the Cross is crushed, before it can even be formulated, by the exterior threat of his neighbours. At the bus station, he feels the need for order and protocol as late arrivals try to push their way ahead to get the best seats. Yet in spite of all these downward movements, this departure is an act of will which lifts Alexandre above his normal life. As the bus leaves Montreal, he is elated: "Que d'espace, de lumière, de liberté" (p. 186). His face happens to be turned away from the prison which he will see on the way back.

The ambiguity which has been present in this departure becomes more pronounced in the arrival and will culminate in the ambiguity of God. Alexandre is lost, pushing his way through the trees in his best suit. He is unable to communicate, unable to remember what suffering brought him there, and uncomfortable with the sensation of peace. He has travelled into another world, where he can look at himself as a stranger. His conscience is also lost and unable to keep up its relentless pursuit. He is free. From confusion there is a sudden climb to contentment, élan, and love of life. The traveller has reached a plateau of satisfaction with God and the world. He takes pleasure in hearing the sound of rain on his cabin roof, welcomes the affection of the farmer's dog and abandons himself to the ancient dream of Robinson Crusoe. He feels no need to explain these feelings. It is the author who reminds her reader discreetly that for a man preoccupied with punctuality and bank accounts, these are signs of the gratuity of life, of love, and of timeless dreams.

The physical basis of the journey is reduced at this stage, but not completely excluded. Alexandre walks through the woods making new discoveries each day. God has filled the woods with fish, game and fruit; He is good, and has made possible a practical paradise on earth. The farmer and his wife are not just another demand on charity like the starving Chinese; they say they are happy with their self-sufficiency. In the mutual pardon of man and God, Alexandre makes the most elevating discovery of all:

—La lune éclairait le sentier. Du reste, Alexandre était maintenant sans frayeur, seul, la nuit, en forêt. Dieu presque toujours lui tenait compagnie ces jours-ci. C'était comme s'il eût pardonné à Alexandre toutes les fautes commises depuis le commencement des siècles.
Mieux encore:
Alexandre éprouva que lui-même, ce soir, en faveur d'Edmondine heureuse, en faveur d'un seul être heureux, pouvait enfin pardonner à Dieu la souffrance jetée si libéralement aux quatre coins du monde. [P. 239]

From this high peak he will fall, not so much by becoming dissatisfied with such a petty happiness as that represented by the farmhouse (that irony is reserved mainly for the reader, and bypasses the character) but by trying to exceed it. The ambiguity of his journey returns in its most excruciating form. The more Alexandre feels elevated, the more he wishes to share his happiness by communicating the discovery to others. As his spirits rise in the discovery of goodness, he is depressed by his impotence in trying to describe it in a letter to the newspaper:

Du lac Vert, il ferait entendre sa voix. Il écrirait. Si possible, il éclairerait. Il devait y avoir un grand nombre d'hommes perplexes, tristes comme il l'avait été lui-même. A ceux-là, Alexandre montrerait le chemin. Il dirait que Dieu veut notre bonheur, et qu'eux-mêmes, les hommes, sont rarement aussi mauvais qu'ils le croient.

. . . .

Il s'assit le dos au lac, face au mur, comme un homme emprisonné.

. . . .

"Cher ami et concitoyen." Rien ne venant à la suite, Alexandre mordilla sa plume. . . . [Pp. 242–46]

In a last attempt to be reasonably happy, Alexandre Chenevert is more successful. He produces two letters and decides to go home. The return journey is a rapid downward motion. Like Sagard's return journey, it contains more human details than the

11839

upward one. The traveller now notices the annoyance of other people, is irritated by the thickening ranks of advertisements, is aware of the prison which he had not noticed as he left Montreal, and worries about traffic accidents. The physical journey expresses completely the rapid spiritual descent from discovery. Back in Montreal, he returns to the need to cross the street safely, to his anxiety for the starving Greeks, and is nauseated by overhearing the hopeful plans of other men to take a trip in the forest. All the details in this chapter sustain the feeling of a rapid descent, until the hero confronts his wife, who comments that he is unchanged. The letter in which he told her to expect a new man is still in his pocket.

The sequence of the whole episode is, then, connected by an actual journey which corresponds in form to the symbolic journey of DesRochers, at the same time as being ironically trite. The journey is essentially a search, and in the spiritual climb more than in the physical, the slow painful ascent and the essential action are to be found. The complete journey is both motion and search. It is a search for both God and man, for some kind of freedom, for peace, and for the resolution of a paradoxical universe. It has ironical pettiness and a personal scale, but it also has a heroic dimension, because the health which Alexandre seeks is, at times, a cure for our sick universe; he is our peer and our champion.

Both the journeys of Alfred DesRochers and Alexandre Chenevert are literary developments of a journey which is, besides having deeper associations, intensely traditional. DesRochers reminds his readers explicitly of the journeys of the lumberjacks and *coureurs de bois*. Alexandre Chenevert's journey on the bus in his best suit is started off by newspaper advertisements containing such words as "camp de trappeur" or "sur l'ancienne piste du Saraguay" (p. 178). Later he will regret that he cannot become a lumberjack. This is the same atavistic memory as that of Alfred DesRochers. It is also confused with the tradition of the farmer's self-sufficiency and moral perfection. When Alexandre thinks of describing himself as a bee-keeper, Gabrielle Roy may be indulging a Virgilian reminiscence. But most of the reminiscences spring from the feeling we have noticed in the pseudo-North of grafting the farmer on to the adventurer. There are frequent references to the idea that God has been good to Canada, and the picture of the Le Gardeur family which Alexandre forms for himself is essentially that of Léo-Paul Desrosiers's novel, *Sources*. There is irony in all this. The author does not really believe that the farm boy's mouth organ supplies artistic satisfaction in the measure which Léo-Paul Desrosiers saw in the return to country life. Nor does she really believe that Alexandre is capable of being any kind of libertine. Yet this memory of tradition is not purely ironic. The call to freedom has a real meaning for Alexandre, and in his two surviving letters there is some memory of his glimpse of moral perfection. These are the core of the positive tradition of the *pays d'en haut*.

The widening of the journey into an odyssey, and the doubling up of the whole of life's journey by means of a final recollection are the evident structure of Gabrielle Roy's latest novel, *La Montagne secrète*. In this novel, the poetic sense of Alfred DesRochers's journey has been more than restored, and the ascent is an artistic elevation. Some sense of imprisonment, more properly a sense of human limitation, is present, but art offers a partial escape from it. The relation of the artist to nature is part of the novelist's aesthetic doctrine, and descriptive passages on *le Grand Nord* are of prime importance in showing it. The whole idea of the journey, scenery, search, danger, courage, freedom, suffering and lonely effort, is a surrealist method of explaining the Canadian artist, and much of it is transposed autobiography.

There is none of the determinism familiar to readers of Gabrielle Roy. With it has gone the painstakingly authentic characterization, giving way to an optimistic simplicity which exceeds that of *La petite Poule d'Eau*, though not retaining its humour. Naturalistic descriptions of the city have been replaced by more or less lyrical attempts to penetrate nature in Ungava and the Mackenzie Valley. Completely absent are the subtle nuances between reality and illusion, between naturalism and symbol, which are the crowning artistic achievement of *Alexandre Chenevert*. In their place are stylized "characters," allegorical narratives, symbols which are clearly contrived to convey a message about the artistic vocation. This simplicity is not always artistically useful.

Yet there is enough in the content of this novel to suggest that it is meant as a summation of Gabrielle Roy's literary quest. In portraying herself as an untutored painter, successful within his own Canadian scene and with his own crude means, she makes what amounts to an important statement about the novel itself. The material she used, the journey, adventure in the wide open spaces and communion with northern nature, are as instinctive and necessary to the Canadian author as the shrubs, animals and people of the North are to her artist.

Cependant le maître venait d'apercevoir aux mains de Pierre une liasse de crayons, que celui-ci ne songeait pas à présenter. Son regard s'anima, il tendit la main pour les recevoir. Aussitôt il fut comme ravi en songe. Ici, rien n'arrêtait l'élan créateur, ne le desservait ni ne le trahissait. Idée, forme, matière, tout cela n'était qu'un; la vision même d'une âme, et cela si clair, si limpide, qu'on y pouvait entrer sans heurt, comme dans la vérité.

Ces chiens au long poil hérissé de neige, leur attitude accablée; ces deux vagues silhouettes de trappeurs vus de dos, se chauffant au maigre confort d'un petit feu allumé sur la neige; autour d'eux cette forêt fragile et tenace; tout cela paraissait vrai; ainsi devenait la vie: dure, inexplicable, d'une misère incompréhensible. Combien de fois en sa vie, se demandait le maître, avait-il vu pareils croquis? tant de vérité jaillir de moyens aussi simples, presque pauvres? Deux ou trois fois, peut-être, et encore!

Il releva les yeux sur Pierre. Celui-ci avait souffert de voir le maître prendre tant d'intérêt aux dessins, choses accomplies avec facilité, tel un jeu, comment auraient-elles pu lui paraître pleines de valeur![8]

The author even seems to be aware of going out of her own territory into new artistic risks, when she shows Pierre Cadorai scorning his drawings for some vast canvas which he can never realize. It is in this light that *La Montagne secrète* is most interesting. It is an imperfect picture of the artist's mission, an attempt to draw an inner portrait of the French-Canadian writer. The very fact that Pierre is something of a *voyageur* shows the importance of the northern journey not as a mere topic, but as a fundamental way of thought. Pierre's portrait draws on most of the accumulated associations of the northern type, and a minimum

[8]Gabrielle Roy, *La Montagne secrète* (Montreal: Beauchemin, 1961), 173–74.

of naturalistic detail lends reality to the figure. It is never related to the novelist's own life—even to the obvious extent of making her picture one of the opposite sex—but uses fragments of "sauvages," *coureurs de bois, voyageurs,* and modern trappers. This primitive artist lives in a society without constraint, which has its own laws responding simply to understood needs. An example of this is the contract between Pierre and his trapping partner, Steve. Made on a few spoken words, understood to end with the season, renewable at mutual convenience, their partnership is too simple to lead to disruption. The term "courir les bois" is used to refer to this life and there is a feeling of freedom in the unlimited country of the trappers. Steve's frank simplicity is an important element in the society preferred by the artist, as is his forest lore. The total impression is of a folk utopia where freedom seems natural.

The artist, like the happy savage, is in harmony with Nature, and there are distinct vestiges of the older figures. Pierre is happy like a savage. His life is perfect simplicity, his wants are few, he can always keep alive in the bush and there is no conflict in the little Republic of men like Steve. Pierre's natural genius is supported by various references to his "chère vie primitive" (p. 139), to his closeness to the "caractère sauvage des rivières du Nord" (p. 178), and to the equation of genius with the term "sauvage" (pp. 136, 158). His first conversation with a tired Parisian art student is like the meeting of a disillusioned eighteenth-century gentleman and a well behaved Huron. His natural happiness is limited only by the human limit; the author expresses this by making him run short of the yellow paint he uses to express warmth and joy. Joy itself is dangerous but in the last resort it is his choice to be consumed for artistic joy. In this sense he is still free and happy, although partly in conflict with Nature.

Essentially free, Pierre finds it hard to submit to the discipline of an art school, though he would like to learn from it. Freedom is a central obsession of his art. From his earliest sketches and wanderings, he has been a man without a predetermined aim, trying by his art to snatch something from the great void. His art could not exist without that freedom from an official goal. It is a human protest, reflecting the struggle of life against a harsh world.

Il arriva à ces mots:
> If thou didst ever hold me in thy heart,
> Absent thee from felicity awhile,
> And in this harsh world draw thy breath in pain,
> To tell my story.

Il releva la tête, se répéta à lui-même: "to tell my story. . . ." Oui, c'était le désir profond de chaque vie, l'appel de toute âme: que quelqu'un se souciât d'elle assez pour s'en ressouvenir quelquefois, et, aux autres, dire un peu ce qu'elle avait été, combien elle avait lutté. [P. 147]

The artist's vital journey is divided into four phases. Pierre is at first wandering uncertainly on the Mackenzie and is aware of his talent. This leads into a second phase, that of seeking some purpose in life higher than keeping alive in a hostile climate. The discovery of the mountain is a physical and spiritual climb; this third phase as a unit corresponds to the type established by Alfred DesRochers. The use of Paris as a symbol of civilized, conscious art, involves an extraneous journey which, however, culminates in imagination and recollection. Thus it recapitulates the previous journeys with a new sense.

The meanderings of the first phase show Pierre as one of the "voyageurs du Grand Nord" (p. 27), travelling in his canoe, living on trapping and fishing, following the appeals of his imagination from place to place. One of these is Fort Renunciation. Without rationalizing his motives, he will sketch Nina, but avoid further relations; later he will hear that she has married his hunting partner. Yet his aim in sacrificing human joy is uncertain. Scenery makes him dimly aware of the artist's mission and his search is echoed in Nina's desire to see the "Big Rockies"; the nomadic urge is a way of expressing imagination and sensibility. As he tries to capture on paper some fragments of his life and quest, he becomes aware of the need of art: "Pour atteindre ce terrible vrai, il commençait à s'en apercevoir, il y a lieu quelquefois de forcer un peu le trait, de souligner" (p. 47).

It is this new demand on him that makes Pierre different, and launches him on the second phase of his search, in which the artistic quest is matched by the "real" events. Trapping with a partner near Lake Caribou, he becomes anxious about his drawings, has to pause for reflection at times of action. He sinks into a despair which corresponds to finding himself a prisoner of blizzards and scurvy. He is released by seeing new qualities in the light of the sun; his partner arrives with coloured crayons, so that he is able to rise to a new level of expression. The triumph is not permanent. Colours present new problems which far exceed his simple means. Returning to the same hunting territory the next winter fails to bring back the same experience; correspondingly, the game has gone further up country. He has to break his partnership, strike out in new directions, seek new departures. A fast stream carries him to the rapids, where he loses his box of mail-order colours. Out of all these ups and downs, however, his new *élan* remains, his renunciation is intact, he is left to seek his way right across the north of Canada.

The third part of his journey is almost a complete unit in itself, and its pattern is similar to that of "Désespérance romantique." In the sequence of the novel it is made to appear as following directly from the break with Steve. In geographical fact, this could hardly be the case, since a canoe journey from the Mackenzie area to Ungava via Flin Flon takes time. However, the link is made by the use of the inhuman, sterile steppe, recalling the break with human associations. The physical journey is an arduous climb through a mineral landscape. The hero is sick and worn out. He is making a difficult portage which lesser men would not have attempted. The way is tortuous and offers no respite. In the mind of the sick hero it recalls previous journeys, struggling towards distant lights which sometimes were hallucination, sometimes cities. He drops with exhaustion, despairing of his artistic mission, wishing he could make the long journey back to being an ordinary man. A new *élan* carries him, beyond the limits of his physical endurance, over the last shoulder, to bring him face to face with a mountain at its most beautiful moment in the sunset. He is at last able to put down his burden and kneel in exaltation.

Physically, Pierre has not climbed the mountain in question, but artistically he is transported to its peak. This is the first part of a mystic elevation, which is developed far more explicitly than any of the others we have dealt with. He is uplifted by emotion in his dialogue with the mountain. There are even a few faint hints of erotic possession in the way he sees it. Some of its rocks rise up like church spires. It is a prodigy of God.

The ascent is followed by a flight into the sublime. After struggling with his limited means to express what he sees in the mountain, he suddenly realizes that he must make a series of paintings of it. The discovery is followed by a sudden approval for something he has done: "il avait fait plus que peindre par étapes la haute montagne glorieuse . . . il avait atteint autre chose encore, de vaste, de spacieux, où il était tel un oiseau à travers l'espace" (p. 112). Like a bird he planes over us; he has left ordinary men, but he has brought them something; the artist is now the primitive hero again, having sacrificed himself for the people. When he frees himself in a realized ecstasy, he is freeing other men.

From these ethereal heights he must fall. He has not yet realized that his work is a challenge to the natural creation, but the author has noted it through the comments of an Eskimo observer. Pierre himself is aware of the insufficiency of what he has actually painted. He detects his soaring ambition, and danger. This brings him back down to the earth of tangible necessities. The artistic vision is ended, and when he returns after at last pursuing food, it will never again be so easily accessible.

Fallen from exaltation into necessity, which he has already avoided longer than is prudent, Pierre trails a lone caribou. This journey is for food, but rapidly develops into another kind of illumination. The circumstances are arranged by the author so that Pierre will wound the animal and then run out of ammunition. He is obliged to pursue his prey and eventually kill it with his bare hands. During the pursuit he identifies himself with the caribou, resting when it is fatigued, thirsting when it stops to drink. The pursuit itself leads through mysterious recesses in the mountains under the insistent light of the moon, a common symbol of subconscious illumination of memory. The killing of the caribou is a horrible moment of truth which will later be described by a more civilized friend as the artist's need to run life into a mould. Pierre's return journey is dark and clouded. Eventually he finds the mountain again, but its face is hidden and his paintings have been damaged by a bear. This oblivion, of course, leads to artistic anguish, which continues on the plane of mystic dialogue between the artist and his mountain. The forebodings and fears and repugnances which he has experienced culminate in failure. He has returned to find his vision terminated, and his imperfect expression of it in shreds, without any hope of completion.

Pierre's anguish is projected again into a physical journey, as he wanders through the Ungava winter, sick and at the mercy of chance. He is brought for recovery to a Distant Early Warning station, and from there the last part of his wanderings will begin. He has been completely expelled from his ingenuous or natural ideal, and will seek to return to it by formal artistic means. The whole pattern of expulsion and return starts off from a semi-realist setting, to finish up in a very stylized Paris-mother-of-the-arts. The implicit literary doctrine is that art draws out of reality something which art will preserve in its own way, and which no longer is reality itself. But behind this is the driving force of the artist's inner vision, in Pierre's case, the mountain, and in Gabrielle Roy's case, the journey.

It is inevitable to relate this to other journeys of expulsion and return. The epic ones have special relevance, since French-Canadian literature was built on racial *mystique* following the Durham Report. It seems very reasonable to argue that the Canadian situation has made this ancient pattern more meaningful and more incumbent on the imagination than it is in modern France. There is no question of its being presented here as a racial epic. Gabrielle Roy has sublimated the struggle for survival into a world of art. The ancient myth to which it bears most resemblance is that of the Grail legends, also to some extent the outcome of a survival propaganda. Pierre, like Sir Perceval, is condemned to suffer and seek to recover a vision which has dispersed.[9] Pierre's arrival in Paris is the most unsatisfactory part of *La Montagne secrète*. It can be seen as an echo of the Arthurian romances, in that the Innocent Fool is now required to go through a series of disciplines (artistic, here, instead of knightly) in order to recover his previously gratuitous vision. However, the result is strained, especially as the author has neither abandoned nor satisfied a desire to make the whole story seem plausible on the natural plane.

---

[9]Cf. George M. Harper, *The Legend of the Holy Grail*, reprint (Baltimore: Modern Languages Association of America, 1893), 8, 13, 14, 30.

The sick hero is eventually led back to his proper territory by the imagination.

> D'où venait que, du simple effort de son esprit, il ressentait plus de fatigue que, naguère, d'avoir porté sur son dos une charge de cent livres, ou d'avoir pagayé à travers de turbulents remous? Il lui arrivait en déposant ses pinceaux de chercher autour de lui d'un air égaré où il se pouvait bien trouver. Auprès du difficile entre tous les fleuves, ce Churchill plein de rapides? L'illusion du portage était si forte qu'il retrouvait le geste d'autrefois pour dégager ses épaules d'un sac pesant. [P. 198]

His early wanderings are recalled through a few surviving sketches. He recaptures enough of himself through this method to feel able to work on a self-portrait. While doing this, he is dying and his suffering recalls the sense of identity he had with the dying caribou stag. Through the stag, he appears to reestablish his identity with the Canadian nature which has always been the source of his art. He is still uncertain of what he is seeking in this last journey:

> Il approchait de son but—l'ignorant encore, mais assuré qu'en le voyant, il le reconnaîtrait. . . .
> Comme autrefois dans l'Ungava, avant que ne lui apparût la montagne étincelante, l'impression lui venait de n'avoir plus que quelques pas à faire pour être ébloui de clarté. L'impression était si forte que, reprenant son pinceau, il lui semblait plutôt soulever son canot, tandis qu'en bas l'eau dangereuse l'attirait. En ces instants de fébrilité, il oubliait jusqu'au pincement de douleur dans sa poitrine. [P. 203]

The self-portrait appears with antlers. This discovery is paralleled in the artistic thesis by Pierre's succeeding for the first time in expressing himself through oils with the same facility as in pencil sketches.

All of this plainly enough repeats the idea of the artist as a sacrificial hero having the terrible privilege of direct communication with Nature. This Nature is both inner and external, united somewhere deep in the soul and never fully separated. Yet external nature, "le monde sauvage de Dieu" (p. 94), is both necessary to the artist and hostile to him. It is in the struggle with and against nature that he realizes himself. He has to be enough detached from Nature to operate on it. This is the source of all art. For the Canadian artist it is most intimately linked with the wild scenery of the North.

Pierre's death is an elevation in which he feels he is again walking through the rough country of Ungava, leaping over obstacles, and rediscovering his mountain. This time his vision of it is perfect. The mountain he now sees is completely his, seen in all lucidity, transformed completely into his own creation. He dies trying to paint a lasting record of it. In sacrificing himself as a man, he is paradoxically liberating man. These are the *élan vital* and protest, which are the real meaning of the *coureur de bois* spirit and the North, applied to literature.

Similar journeys are to be found in other novels and poems in which a hero has to seek a higher truth beyond the pale of socially accepted man. In all cases other than *rayonnement* literature, and even in the best of that, the northern journey entails a serious commitment to freedom. Consequently, it has proved a very appropriate imaginative setting for literature of social and metaphysical revolt. Involvement with nature has also been one of the permanent features of the northern journey, and adds intensity to the revolt as created by André Langevin and Yves Thériault as well as Gabrielle Roy. Nature in its most ambiguous sense has also led many writers to echo, in works set in the *pays d'en haut*, man's ineradicable attempt to return to the purer nature sometimes associated with the myth of the noble savage. These possibilities, already mentioned in this chapter, will be treated more fully in the next two. They are, nevertheless, inseparable from the artistic vision of the journey *en haut*.

The culmination of this artistic vision in the journey of an artist towards his goal of perfect expression is the logical conclusion of the whole tradition. On the one hand, there was little before *La Montagne secrète* to show that the *voyageur* type in literature was on his way to becoming an artist. On the other hand, there was everything to show that this was his destiny. Pierre Cadorai, like Alfred DesRochers, feels as he takes up the instrument of his artistic expression, that his back in bending under the weight of a *voyageur*'s pack. For when the French-Canadian artist sets out on his search, it is most likely that he will remember the adventures of the *pays d'en haut* legend. In the journey itself, and in its baffling discovery, the writer finds ready food for his imagination. The survival of traditional elements is therefore to be found in places quite apart from the deliberate historical cult of the *rayonnement* writers. Alexandre Chenevert and Pierre Cadorai continue different aspects of Alfred Des-Rochers's sublimated lumberjack. It is equally true, though less immediately evident, that these all echo the early contact with the Canadian forest which is best (but not solely) expressed by Sagard. The reason seems to be that Sagard, more than any other recorded traveller *en haut,* got sufficiently lost to let his inner preoccupations stamp their form on the outward journey. The freedom and nature he was exploring were not in Huronia, not in the forest, but in himself, excited by these outward tokens. That is the elementary appeal of the Canadian forest which has not changed, because the modern man setting out into it is still taking with him the same unsatisfied desire to balance order and freedom, and the same yearning to confront and interrogate something more absolute than the fragile realities of his real habitat.

CHAPTER FIVE

Regeneration

Freedom, as it was understood by the early observers of the *pays d'en haut*, is mainly divisible into licence and the spirit of liberty. For the former, Sagard is most remembered. His terse, factual accounts of the sexual behaviour of the Hurons give way to scandalized comments. Yet these do not quite conceal an amused tolerance:

. . . il arrive souuent que telle passe ainsi sa ieunesse, qui aura eu plus de douze ou quinze marys, tous lesquels ne sont pas neantmoins seuls en la iouyssance de la femme, quelques mariez qu'ils soient: car la nuict venuë les ieunes femmes et filles courent d'une Cabane à autre, comme font, en cas pareil, les ieunes hommes de leur costé, qui en prennent par où bon leur semble, sans aucune violence toutesfois, remettant le tout à la volonté de la femme. Le mary fera le semblable à sa voysine, et la femme à son voysin, aucune jalousie ne se mesle entr'eux pour cela, et n'en reçoiuent aucune honte, infamie ou des-honneur.

. . . .

Une des grandes et plus fascheuses importunitez qu'ils nous donnoient au commencement de nostre arriué en leur pays, estoit leur continuelle poursuitte et prieres de nous marier, ou du moins de nous allier auec eux, et ne pouuoient comprendre nostre maniere de vie Religieuse: à la fin ils trouuerent nos raisons bonnes, et ne nous importunerent plus, approuuans que ne fissions rien contre la volonté de nostre bon Pere Iesus; et en ces poursuittes les femmes et filles estoient, sans comparaison, pires et plus importunes que les hommes mesmes, qui venoient nous prier pour elles.[1]

He was much more censorious of the French libertines who were corrupting the savages:

. . . elles commençoient à avoir de la retenuë, et quelque honte de

---

[1] Gabriel Sagard, *Le Grand Voyage du pays des Hurons*, 3rd ed. (Toronto: The Champlain Society, 1939), 336; M 165–7.

leur dissolution, n'osans plus, que fort rarement, vser de leurs imper-
tinentes paroles en nostre presence, et admiroient, en approuuant
l'honnesteté que leur disions estre aux filles de France, ce qui nous
donnoient esperance d'vn grand amendement, et changement de
leur vie dans peu de temps: si les François qui estoient montez auec
nous (pour la pluspart) ne leur eussent dit le contraire pour pouuoir
tousiours iouyr à cœur saoul, comme bestes brutes, de leurs char-
nelles voluptez, ausquelles ils se veautroient, iusques à auoir en
plusieurs lieux des haras de garces, tellement que ceux qui deuoient
seconder à l'instruction et bon exemple de ce peuple, estoient ceux-
là mesme qui alloient destruisans et empeschans le bien que nous
establissions au salut de ces peuples, et à l'aduancement de la gloire
de Dieu. [P. 340; M 177–8]

Corruption implies initial innocence. There is a hint that this was
to be found in moral neutrality: in their relations with one
another the Hurons felt no proper shame and no sinful joy.

. . . [les jeunes Hurons] ont licence de s'adonner au mal si tost qu'ils
peuuent, et les ieunes filles de se prostituer si tost qu'elles en sont
capables, voir mesme les peres et meres sont souuent maquereaux
de leurs propres filles: bien que ie puisse dire auec vérité, n'y auoir
iamais veu donner un seul baiser, ou faire aucun geste ou regard
impudique: et pour cette raison i'ose affermer qu'ils sont moins
suiets à ce vice que par deçà. . . . [P. 334; M 160]

Joy and shame were the gifts of civilization, whereas nature
taught only simple good things:

Nonobstant que les femmes se donnent carriere auec d'autres qu'auec
leurs marys, et les marys auec d'autres qu'auec leurs femmes, si est-ce
qu'ils ayment tous grandement leurs enfans, gardans cette Loy que
la Nature a entée és cœurs de tous les animaux, d'en auoir le soin.
[P. 336; M 167]

Sagard did not follow this argument to any general conclusion.
However, the picture he left was undoubtedly attractive. Elabo-
rated on by Lahontan and Diderot at a later date, it was to enjoy
a considerable vogue in Paris, where "souffler l'allumette" became
a byword for free love.[2]

The spirit of liberty is a more serious objection. Sexual licence
could be regarded as a mere excess of a human weakness, but
free thinking was potentially an attack on the one authority which

[2]Gilbert Chinard, *L'Amérique et le rêve exotique* . . . *au XVIIe et au
XVIIIe siècle* (Paris: Droz, 1934), 232. The expression is from Lahontan,
and supposed to denote a phase in Huron courtship.

Sagard never questioned, the Christian revelation. The objection goes deeper. Liberty is insidious because it is an attractive quality, connected by Sagard himself with the natural goodness he found in the savages. He was, of course, inconsistent. He admired liberty in political and economic matters, but condemned it in family relations and general outlook. This led him into subordinate contradictions, such as his statement that "il n'y a point de respect des jeunes aux vieils" (p. 338; M 173) as against his picture of authority based on respect for elders (Ch. 17). His feelings were undoubtedly mixed, as must have been the feelings of every Frenchman in the land.

The concept of nature provides the best answer to Sagard's distinction between good and bad freedom. He admired the Huron family wherever he could see it as a self-binding system. Parents' eventual dependence on their children reinforced natural love and supported purposeful procreation. This was good, according to his implicit logic, because the bonds of nature are not opposed to good freedom, as the unnatural bonds of money and authority are. Yet he was aware of the contempt with which the Hurons greeted the idea of monogamy, and he condemned their arguments for the individual's right to choose any mate that pleased at almost any time. Here, religious teaching was needed to supplement the good of Nature.

"Ils sont libertins, et ne demandent qu'à iouër et se donner du bon temps" (p. 339; M 175), is probably Sagard's conclusion. Nevertheless, the undercurrent of love and admiration is inescapable. The lasting impression is of the proud savage untrammelled by worldly cares, enjoying the freedom which men like Sagard dreamed of. The missionary's regret at being recalled to Paris instead of left to do what he most wanted is evident and there is no reason to doubt that he resented the political successes of the rival Jesuit Order. In the last analysis, only such feelings are reliable guides to the real meaning. In spite of contradictions, the *Grand Voyage* shows that even before the influence of the *philosophes* and satirists, there was a distinct feeling that the savages were in some ways morally superior to Frenchmen, superior to them in the enjoyment of life, in physique, courage, generosity and dignity. On the whole their superiority was due to their freedom.

Missionaries also had various doctrinal and practical reasons for fostering the image of the good savage. The Jesuits as a whole were influenced by Molinism, which sought evidence of God's grace in human nature itself. There had to be a human nature in which some goodness, though recognizable to Europeans, was not due to their teaching or customs. Such views were supported by the needs of foreign missions. Firstly, there was a need to curb the profiteers who regarded South American Indians as beasts of burden; the dignity of the savage had to be defended. Secondly, there was a need to accomplish statistical wonders of conversion without waiting for the Christian way of thinking to be absorbed; a "natural" predisposition to understand Christian mysteries was a useful device. Thirdly, fund-raising propaganda demanded a certain optimism; it is also probable that many missionaries had to fight hard to convince themselves of the good of their campaign, as they watched the evils of civilization spread more rapidly than its virtues. Fourthly, those evils had to be preached against, and the virtuous savage was an excellent rhetorical figure with which to reproach the wayward European.

The persistent illusion of the happy man of nature is still to be found. If it can survive into the middle of the present century, and still override factual observation, we should be less surprised at its foundations in the seventeenth and eighteenth centuries. Mgr Gabriel Breynat, a missionary with fifty years' experience, mostly among Chipewyan Indians in the Mackenzie District, gives proof of this survival. Among his Indians he found simple piety, childlike honesty, natural awareness of the Creator and lack of foresight in material concerns. Many of his anecdotes and explanations conform very badly to such a characterization. Yet he confidently offers a sentimental synthesis:

—rois et maîtres en leurs forêts vierges, que ne leur disputait encore aucune cupidité . . . nomades intrépides . . . heureux et fiers, l'âme sereine . . . peu soucieux du lendemain.[3]

Curiously suggestive of the way myths of this kind are transmitted, this synthesis is not original. The writer is quoting from the work of another missionary, Sister Paulette Fortier. The use

[3]Quoted in *Chez les Mangeurs de caribou* by Gabriel Breynat (Montreal: Fides, 1945), 19. This volume is the first of a trilogy under the general title *Cinquante Ans au pays des neiges.*

of the savage as a scourge for the civilized also continues. The English-Canadian writer, Farley Mowat, provides a good example of how far this principle can develop its own higher mysteries when he says:

Let moralists peddle their wares to those who would think of the Innuit as barbaric . . . but let them keep their sanctimonious mouthings from the ears of . . . those . . . who alone know what it is to assist death in his work.[4]

It is probably Gabrielle Roy who best sums up the main principle of the inextinguishable happy savage, when she shows Alexandre Chenevert dreaming of the bliss of Indonesians and Eskimos.[5] Nostalgia for "natural" bliss will always occur when the social animal laments his human condition.

Gilbert Chinard has demonstrated that the noble savage is just this kind of myth, with roots deep in European thought.[6] The American experience gave it new life and new substance, which certainly affected imaginations in France. In Canada, on the other hand, the Frenchman's nostalgia for freedom and bliss could not remain indefinitely attached to the real Indians. Through the general feeling about the *pays d'en haut*, this French dream was transferred to the new social type, the *coureur de bois*.

The *coureur de bois* was a more real and more protean character in the minds of the colonists. His elusive presence is everywhere. As we have already suggested, the *coureurs de bois* were partly assimilated to the life and character of the Indians. Affranchised from the excessive controls of the colonial church and government, yet not subjected to the social restrictions of their Indian hosts, they indeed seemed free, happy mortals. They were civilized men who had successfully returned to nature, it seemed. Their dependence on trade notwithstanding, the *coureurs de bois* were a kind of happy savage, and heirs to both the abhorrence and admiration that the savage inspired. Duchesneau and

[4]Farley Mowat, *People of the Deer* (London: Michael Joseph, 1952), 179.
[5]Gabrielle Roy, *Alexandre Chenevert* (Montreal: Beauchemin, 1954), 176, 272.
[6]Gilbert Chinard, *L'Exotisme américain . . . au XVIe siècle* (Paris: Hachette, 1911).

Charlevoix both denounced them for their obdurate attachment to liberty.

The new lords of the forest enjoyed a freedom which ranged from licentious behaviour to civil disobedience in the matter of trade. They were unaccountably able to defy the Church on certain points of conduct, and eventually the representatives of absolute sovereignty had to meet them half way. In spite of prohibitions, they were able to swagger in front of the law-abiding public and occupy a place in the popular imagination.

The *coureur de bois* proper occupies surprisingly little space in French-Canadian literature. The romantic figure of Du Luth has not been given the prominence of the sacrificial hero, Dollard des Ormeaux. François-Xavier Garneau and Lionel Groulx, whom we take as the best two examples of history firing creative imaginations, both give Du Luth very scant mention. Garneau accepted in good faith the documents he had read, and so gives a sketch of an outlaw, such as Duchesneau might have dictated. It was the American writer, Francis Parkman, who made the most of the *coureurs de bois*. Yet the author of the Preface to Alexandre-Antonin Tachés *Vingt Années* was able to exclaim in 1888:

> Ah! on chante le coureur des bois!
> Au spectacle de cet homme fantastique—héros très souvent par caprice—qui s'élance à la poursuite des aventures ou des richesses . . . la lyre du poète vibre et s'émeut.[7]

He describes their journeys as a mixture of plains, forests, rivers and songs. Whatever vibrant poets he was referring to, they evidently admired the *coureur de bois*, probably confused him completely with the *voyageur*, and generally romanticized him. On the other hand, they did not overlook the elements of caprice which were essential to his character, and are a form of freedom. The legend was still growing, because it was irrevocably attached to the image of the *pays d'en haut*.

The sum total constitutes a type, part literary, part folk, which is a living force in French-Canadian writers, whether they identify it by name with *coureurs de bois* or not. This type does overlap, in some of its essential qualities, with that of the early pioneer,

[7]M. T. A. Bernier, preface to Alexandre-Antonin Taché, *Vingt Années*, 9.

whose posterity in patriotic literature is well known. Both had striking universal skills, both were made by these into "natural" possessors of land, both are examples of how best to enjoy life. The essential difference is that in one all these qualities are co-ordinated by a vision of perfection, to which the character conforms as if to a higher authority; in the other these qualities are kept alive by the vitality of a freedom which defies or ignores authority. These two types may conveniently be termed "soft" and "hard," since they clearly parallel the hard and soft savages distinguished by Lovejoy, Boas and their associates.[8] Their similarities and opposition echo the bi-polarity of early Canadian geography, as well as French conflicts on the question of human nature. Nowadays it is easy to see that the "soft" type is based on a fixed vision of human nature, whereas the "hard" type lends itself to existential thinking. This is the reason for the re-emergence of the latter type in recent literature. The "soft" type, and the deliberate confusion by which he appropriated qualities from his Esau-like brother, were more favoured by Victorian idealism. In both cases, however, the types have a deeper history than the influences which have brought them out in their respective periods.

From the *coureur de bois* to the *voyageur* and ultimately the lumberjack there is a real historical sequence (see chapter 1). In literature these social types inherit some of the characteristics which the *coureurs de bois* acquired from the happy savage. Diluted, converted and metamorphosed, these have a continuity down to Alfred DesRochers and beyond. The result is that some vestiges of the happy savage survive as a French-Canadian literary tradition. A series of standard figures, displaying combinations of a list of standard qualities, are related to each other through this common origin. The figures, which sometimes occur in combination and are not all of the same literary importance, are: the persisting happy savage, a modified Indian, the pioneer, the bushman, the canoeman, the *Métis*, the trapper, the missionary, the lumberjack, the aimless wanderer, the adulteress, the artist, and the ancestor. The qualities fall into less rigid categories, but may be provisionally listed as: proximity to external

[8]Arthur O. Lovejoy, George Boas and others, *Primitivism and Related Ideas in Antiquity* (Baltimore: Johns Hopkins Press, 1935), 10.

nature, physical strength and beauty, vitality, natural possession of land, courage, skill, spiritual awareness, and superiority to morals. Generally, they represent some kind of protest, which in modern literature has developed into a full-blown revolt.

The main link in this transmission of the libertine spirit is *Forestiers et voyageurs*. Although Joseph-Charles Taché, a man of reactionary authoritarian ideas, plainly intended to make his *voyageur* into a vehicle for the idea of *rayonnement* through the common people of French Canada, he did not altogether succeed in suppressing the other features of the *pays d'en haut* legend. Indeed, he could not, for he was also attempting, in the best tradition of the Patriotic School, to preserve the picture of an authentic French-Canadian folk type. The result is exactly what he declares in his preface: folklore adapted to polite taste, which in 1863 meant conformity to a doctrinaire outlook. The characterization of the composite *voyageur* type divides fairly easily into two sides, the pious and the libertine, which correspond to "soft" and "hard." They come together in a vision of natural goodness which seems to account for the perfection of Père Michel either way.

Père Michel's story begins with the account of his own baptism, which was celebrated to such effect that his godmother quite failed to notice that she had dropped the baby in a snowdrift. Such is the stuff *voyageurs* were made of, and the verve of its telling shows that the story does not belie the character of the folk narrator, even if Taché does feel obliged to end with a plea for temperance. After passing through an apprenticeship of poaching, Père Michel took to the *pays d'en haut* to evade the law. Despite his moralizing intentions, Taché had to show his *voyageur* as a gay outlaw in accordance with the legend which started, as we have seen, with the *coureurs de bois*.

It was necessary to Taché's thesis to show that the new recruit fitted naturally into his new occupation, being endowed with a set of natural untaught skills, simple piety, spontaneous happiness, ownership of vast domains by a law beyond laws, and a goodness which, even if incapable of preventing the hero from killing a man, compensates both him and us spiritually. There is also enough evidence of partial assimilation to Indians to reinforce the link with men of nature. The obvious inconsistencies in this scheme are partly a heritage of the original noble savage myth, partly the result of social propaganda in the work of the Quebec School.

Closeness to nature is a constant quality of Taché's ideal *voyageur*, which is first outlined and then created in Père Michel, François, a few minor characters, and the general association of other material which is delivered to the reader through Michel's narrative. Impressive physique and good health are the outward signs of natural advantages. Like Duchesneau's *coureurs de bois*, these men look like the flower of French-Canadian manhood. They have an understanding of nature which is evident throughout the story in their fishing and trapping skills. They can read tracks in the snow as other men might read a book. Through observing tracks and other signs, they tell the author stories of animals which remind him of La Fontaine. Communion with Nature leads to a higher truth than the reason of "les esprits forts." Taché is, however, a little uneasy about his claim to see folk wisdom in goblin stories, and concludes: "jouissons-en en tout cas comme de conceptions poétiques qui touchent au côté mystérieux de notre être."[9] On the other hand, he does make other claims for intuitive wisdom. In the course of the narrative, he assures the reader that Père Michel,

avec la science du petit catéchisme pour base et sa longue et honnête expérience des choses de la création, avait des solutions admirables pour bien des questions philosophiques qui ont tourné la tête à beaucoup de malheureux soi-disant penseurs. [P. 134]

He adds that he has known many common men

chez qui une foi sincère, une grande honnêteté de but et le contact continuel avec la nature, servis par beaucoup d'intelligence, ont fait fleurir et fructifier cette précieuse semence des vérités naturelles restées dans l'homme après sa chute. [P. 134]

The remark last quoted, relating the near-perfection of the *voyageur* to the Fall, relates it to all happy savage myths. True, it has been adapted so as to avoid making the hero into an unfallen man, but the feeling is plainly that some are more

[9]J-C Taché, *Forestiers et voyageurs*, 2nd ed. (Montreal: Fides, 1946), 89.

unfallen than others. They are protected by their contact with nature, from which they draw understanding that is both salutory and practical.

The characterization in some parts of the story makes considerable humour out of the popular tendency towards superstition, which is felt to be a harmless concomitant of simple piety. The unconverted Indians are superstitious, too. This leads to the interesting question of resemblance between them and the *voyageur* type. The author probably did not intend this similarity, but could not resist it because it gave rise to humour in many episodes. His picture of Père Michel crossing himself to ward off the devil conjured by his Indian hunting partner is good innocent fun because his belief in his own signs is equalled by his belief in those of the heathen. It all corresponds to the naturally religious disposition which the Jesuits had been wont to find in savages. This is also present in *Forestiers et voyageurs*:

Ce qu'il y a de beau et de bon chez les Montagnais, c'est que les enfants apprennent leurs prières, leur catéchisme et le chant même, sans que le missionaire s'en mêle presque. [P. 114]

The character, Père Michel, is in some respects aware of his proximity to Indian life, and subscribes to the happy savage theory. It would be a serious misunderstanding of the author's purpose if we lost sight of the humorous bent of his story-teller, or of the real difference between Michel and his Indian friends, symbolized by the eventual return to his parish steeple which he is supposed never to forget. He will always be restrained from "going bush" by an ulterior notion of Christian duty which outweighs immediate visions of happiness. With the principle of duty in mind, we can see the humorous point of the author's sending his character a temptation to which many, as he admits, succumbed.

To complete the picture of Joseph-Charles Taché's *voyageur* as a new happy savage, it remains to be said that he is happy. His happiness is most readily visible in a spontaneous and apparently endless stream of either song or story-telling. The author provides several examples of the folk songs, which on the whole are gay and make light of the sufferings of the journey. Their rustic fun, such as the "baptism" of new recruits, is also described. Of course, we have some difficulty in believing that these spontaneous expressions of gaiety were so continuous in view of the physical conditions and the prospects of long isolation. However, the real point about the *voyageur*'s happiness is that he is in harmony with his own world and with himself. Satisfied by the activities which are proper to him, he seeks nothing beyond his station. He fulfils his own nature and has no unsatisfied cravings. His world is complete so long as no rival form of trading disrupts it. That world is almost entirely the world of the *pays d'en haut*.

Taché's fusion of the *coureur de bois* type with the *rayonnement* hero described in the last chapter was fairly common in the nineteenth century. Louis Fréchette and A-G Morice, as we have noted, lumped all evidence of French presence together indiscriminately. Anybody who had been in the bush had to qualify as "Humbles soldats de Dieu, sans reproche et sans crainte, / Qui portiez le flambeau de la vérité sainte," to support the thesis of a vigorously spreading French Catholic civilization. The expansive vitality associated with the *pays d'en haut* was needed just as much in retrospect as it had been needed in fact in the days of Louis XV. Taché's portrait shows that the reasons for this go deeper than mere survival propaganda. Just like the "hard" and "soft" savages behind them, the idealized or legendary figures of the *voyageur* and the pioneer have always been subject to a certain confusion when the real figures were not distinct enough to prevent it. At the time Taché came to know the forest men of Rimouski, there was a real convergence of *voyageur* lumberjacks and pioneer lumberjacks. It was natural to bring them together in one concept of human perfection, which in itself was inspired partly by political feeling and partly by our endless nostalgia for an idyllic nature.

The adventurous rogue survives in *Forestiers et voyageurs*, in spite of his fusion with the pious conformist. He survives without such fusion in the writings of G. Dugas, a *pays d'en haut* missionary who knew at first hand the *voyageurs* who did not return to the village steeple. In his *Un Voyageur des pays d'en haut* (1890) he states that most of them in fact could not return to Canada because they were too far away and too attached to their new life. His general explanation supports the idea that the *voyageur* was closely allied in spirit to the *coureur de bois* or "hard" type:

La seule explication possible de ce goût étrange qui faisait abandonner si gaiement la vie civilisée pour la vie sauvage, était l'amour d'une liberté sans contrôle.[10]

The core of the type is the same inconsequential freedom which Alexandre-Antonin Taché found in the *Métis*, and Sagard in the Hurons. It is evident in the character study of *Un Voyageur*, and also in Dugas(t)'s *La Première Canadienne du Nord-Ouest*, a biography of the first white woman whose husband was irresponsible enough to take her buffalo hunting. Notwithstanding the many adventures to which he exposed his legal spouse, such as meeting his Indian concubine, or giving birth in a buffalo herd, Jean-Baptiste Lagimonière seems to have been proof against any kind of moralizing, and maintained in fact the freedom from civilized cares which legend associates with his type.

Other scattered evidence of the popularity of the "hard" natural types is to be found in the works of Claude-Henri Grignon and Léo-Paul Desrosiers, where they are also seen as indispensable adjuncts of vitality. In *Les Opiniâtres*, Desrosiers shows François, the first son of an early French settler, as the man who saved the settlement because he was able to adapt himself to Indian skills in hunting, canoeing and warfare. Although he worried his father by going half native, he is shown as the hero of the day and the necessary counterpart to the sedentary farming types. Grignon's Alexis, a minor character in *Un Homme et son péché*, is the twentieth-century lumberjack who has settled down to farming but is not quite in his element. He is there mainly as a foil to his cousin Séraphin, the miser, whose success depends on a rigid discipline. Alexis is considered to be something of a libertine in the village, where Séraphin is generally respected for his riches. The novel, however, makes it abundantly plain that the miser represents sterility and death, whereas the lumberjack represents love, generosity and life.

The same sense clearly attaches to the ancestral figures of Alfred DesRochers's nostalgic journeys. Their central quality is

[10]G. Dugas(t), *Un Voyageur des pays d'en haut*, 2nd ed. (Montreal: Beauchemin, 1912), 11.

usually vigour or freedom or both in close unison. The brutality of certain scenes emphasizes the fact that their affinity with nature belongs in the "hard" category. The studied ugliness of certain descriptions—the tannery, the muddy potato pickers, the slaughter of a pig—remind us that the ancestor, like most "hard" savages including Sagard's Hurons, excites nostalgia but is not offered as a pattern for exact emulation. To be effective, the literary savage has to be beyond our reach, and the uncouthness of his vigour is the most effective barrier. The external nature with which this ancestor figure is inextricably linked is typically hard and teeming with life. The central figure of his "Paysage sylvestre" is a playful bear, and it looks very like some of the poet's backwoods ancestors.

Some aspects of the composite type of Alfred DesRochers are the main features of Thomas Clarey, in Bertrand Vac's *Louise Genest*. He is an eloquent lover, drawing much of his attraction from direct participation in the Nature of the forest. He belongs to the social type which continues to survive in the forest, both resisting and adapting itself to the encroachment of business. He is strong, hard and morally ambiguous. He is felt on the whole to be superior to the men of the village both in goodness and happiness, though he is not a spotless ideal, and with him we have to accept some of the cruelty of nature.

Through details including special vocabulary, Bertrand Vac has related his trapper to the main lineage of the type. He uses the term, "courir les bois" in a derogatory sense for the life they lead; Thomas Clarey uses the term "en haut" to indicate the life beyond the villagers, in the forest or in the Indian Reserve. Clarey himself is in fact a *Métis*, has lived with his mother on the Reserve, has learned his hunting skills from an uncle and refers to himself as "sauvage" in character.

To this we can add a few characteristics common to the legendary noble savage and *coureur de bois*. Clarey's physique is frequently mentioned. It expresses the health of the man of nature, the joy of his activity, and a simple, natural grace which is contrasted with the appearance of Louise's husband. The trapper is simple and self-sufficient. Improvident, he does not foresee the problems which must follow his association with Louise. His basic needs are attended to by himself, and others do not arise. This gives him an inner calm, on which Louise at the height of her crisis can comment: "La simplicité spontanée qui était sienne ignorait les introspections et les complications."[11] This is not completely true, for he is also superstitious; a fallen pine dashes his happiness.

On the whole he shows common sense in difficult situations, limited only by a lack of understanding of some of Louise's sensibilities. These would not normally enter into his life, since they are due to a society which is not natural.

Thomas Clarey is happy and good. As with the original happy savages, these terms need some qualification. Yet this does not diminish the major feeling of happiness and goodness in either case, and through that feeling this modern trapper is linked to the essential happy savage type. His happiness and goodness are interdependent, and are built upon his individual freedom and his vital contact with Nature.

His happiness is mainly a form of contentment. He has no interest in Armand Genest's desire for money and political influence. When he is faced with a complicated crisis, it does not concern him because it is based on the conflict of values which belong to society and are not his. Yet there is a positive side to his happiness. He is able to communicate it to Louise. In the course of his life he has struggled through enough alien ways of living to know that the forest and the men of the forest are his home, and that they fill his life with satisfying activity.

Freedom is an essential of this activity. However hard and strenuous it may be, however cruel some of his contact with nature, his life is like the play of the otter, unconstrained, self-sufficient and almost unconscious: "Je fais ce que je veux quand je veux" (p. 14), "Il n'y a rien comme de vivre à son goût" (p. 17). "Vis pour toi, maintenant" (p. 66), he advises Louise, and his own relation with her illustrates the point. The whole plot of the novel is built on his uncomplicated rejection of the social order and Louise's complicated attempt to escape from it. For both of them society seems to mean men like Armand Genest, who is rich, tyrannical, unfeeling, unpleasant, and a churchwarden. Thomas feels that its law is an abuse:

[11]Aimé Pelletier (pseud. Bertrand Vac), *Louise Genest* (Montreal: Le Cercle du Livre de France, 1950), 130.

Mais de quel droit cet idiot de Genest tient-il sa femme dans la maison? Parce qu'il est allé devant le curé, jurer de lui être fidèle jusqu'à la mort? [P. 22]

Triumphant, he is able to be more tolerant but no less subversive:

—Il ne faut pas trop lui en vouloir, dit-il enfin. Il n'est pas le seul responsable, tu sais. A l'école, quand on y va, on nous apprend l'histoire sainte et le catéchisme. Après, on se marie au plus vite, on fait des enfants, puis on trime. Plus tard, quand il y en a un qui n'est pas heureux et se met à courir, on le montre du doigt. [P. 50]

This rather petulant revolt against the narrowness of society becomes more serious when we realize that society itself wages war on men like Clarey, just as it did in the days when intendants tried to tie men to the soil by interdictions and early marriage. His hunting territory is threatened by the advances of a paper company. All the life of freedom and happiness he has built will in any case be demolished in a few years.

In all the realist details of life in the forest, Bertrand Vac shows a traditional man comparable with Joseph-Charles Taché's *forestiers*. His simplicity, satisfaction, frankness, charm and so on would fit either pattern. Clarey is the man of universal skills who can make moccasins and snowshoes, who can go anywhere with his dog-team or canoe, who can keep alive by his own skill and ingenuity. He reads the ground and the sky like a book, and can tell Louise stories of what has happened near his traps. He is the perfect hunter, identified with his prey, the otter. Its characteristic playfulness is written in his own character.

The author supplements Clarey by the addition of other backwoods types. Père Jobin and Père André are two picturesque characters based, according to Bertrand Vac's prefatory remark, on real individuals. Jointly, they are kindly, tolerant, temperate old backwoods sages, unmistakeable folk types of the same kind as J-C Taché's *François le veuf*. They could not exist elsewhere. Jobin originally came from Montreal but it is hinted that he had good cause for taking to the bush. Père André particularly is the man of the woods, with the local colour of a folk type. These and the other men of the forest form a community with its own cohesion and harmony. But here the resemblance with Taché ends, for it is not a hierarchical society. Jobin, a fugitive from

115

the law, and André, sympathetic to the adulterous pair, speak for a society based on freedom. There is no law but that of nature. Partnership is a general rule for mutual advantage, with a faint hint of government by elders. But men are free to make exceptions, even if this will not result in lasting success. It is in this kind of society, a compromise between nature and civilization, that the reader is mostly made to feel the goodness of natural men including Thomas Clarey: "Dans le bois, on laisse les portes ouvertes . . . Grandes ouvertes! Tout le monde est bienvenu" (p. 42). The picture is not devoid of sentimentalism.

The character of Thomas Clarey is constantly related to nature, both in the sense of "being natural" and of being close to external nature, as in his identification with the otter. There is here a striking reversal of J-C Taché's false precept that all the *voyageurs* returned to their parish steeple. "Tous les coureurs de bois vont en ville un jour ou l'autre, mais ils reviennent tous, tôt ou tard," says Clarey (p. 88). It is Nature which paradoxically commands their fidelity and gives them their freedom.

The novel contains descriptions of the forest which are pretty, Romantic or vaguely Franciscan. Their main purpose is to create the impression of fulness of life. But these are not by any means the complete picture of external nature to which Bertrand Vac's hero corresponds. "Vis comme tu voudras," warns Père André, "mais n'oublie pas le bois, c'est dangereux" (p. 63). The nature which offers freedom, then, has some strict demands of its own. Its cruel severity is repeated in various ways, preparatory to the conclusion where Louise and her son perish. The forest can become a nightmare, in which men lose their senses. When Louise looks to it for a moral rule, she finds ambiguity everywhere: mothers in nature do not desert their young, but risk everything to protect them; yet young animals leave their mothers to make their own life (p. 110). The only rule that experienced forest men know is: "Quand on a peur, on est fini" (p. 103). This is exactly the case with both Louise and her son.

Thomas Clarey shares the severity of the forest with which he lives, and he survives, ready to find another mate, just as the forest returns to its oblivious calm after swallowing Louise. So long as she could live with him naturally he was gentle and strong. When she was unable to accept the way of nature, she was lost. Like the folk type shown by Alfred DesRochers, Clarey has virtues which are not transferable into the system of civilized values, just as the forest offers life without any fundamental possibility of compromise with society.

Louise is a more human character, because, though she is at odds with the society in which she lives, she cannot completely abandon its values. Through this conflict, the novel acquires its tragic element, and the theme of Nature in man acquires its pathos. In that she falls in love with Thomas Clarey and has a loathsome business-like husband, Louise Genest is a woman trying to return to nature. Having finally gone to live with the trapper, she succeeds in rejecting both past and future and in living for the day. The parish priest, who understands her problems, shows that this is the real opposition between his law and her life: "Vous avez eu tort de désirer le bonheur ici-bas" (p. 144). This will lead her to question God as well as the sacrament she has violated: "On ne vit qu'une fois" (p. 164) is still the core of her protest.

The author is at pains to give innocence to Louise's break with society and its conventions. Her life in the village is made to seem as unhealthy (morally) as possible. The beginnings of her association with the *Métis* are innocent and spread over six years. Their journey up to his camp, on a stream beneath birds and boughs in bud, reminds her of a childhood nostalgia. Her adultery is first presented as an absorption of his moral neutrality. "Suivant les principes du métis, Louise se laissa vivre sans résistance" (p. 53). What she has cast off is mainly the unpleasantness of the village, in order to come closer to the bliss of nature. She is trying to live up to his remark: "Quand on vit dans le bois, plus on s'en rapproche et mieux on le connaît, plus c'est facile" (p. 53). So it should be with her moral state. By understanding and accepting that she has chosen the good, the natural life, by resigning herself to complete loss of the social values she has abandoned, she should be innocent and happy. However, this state is not attained. When she observes mother animals, she looks for the rule of duty, not for the rule of survival. Eventually Louise loses even belief in her original innocence, as well as being rejected by nature. Looking back on earlier events, she can see only guilt: she had clung to Genest for the security of his money, she was at fault in wanting a happiness he could not give, she had subconsciously engineered the crisis that drove her into the woods with her trapper. Although the element of revolt in this novel is mostly social, the overall impression of Louise's destruction is that it was the inevitable outcome of a metaphysical conflict.

Roger Lemelin's *Pierre le magnifique* contains passing reference to the lumberjack legend. Lemelin's topic is Quebec city and its popular ideals. But a lumber camp episode is an essential part of that topic. In the narrative, it is the starting point of Pierre's rise to independence and power. The forest is a place of freedom and strong men. It is accepted that Pierre is there because he has had to run away from authority. The reader's first view of him as a lumberjack reveals that he is free to read Karl Marx.

In order to fulfil the ideal of the popular hero which he is ironically constructing, Lemelin has to make Pierre go through a lumberjack sequence. His rugged athletic appearance is part of the requirement, but its superficiality is picked out by all the incidents. When Pierre is eventually roused to action, his behaviour is dictated by what he remembers seeing at the cinema, and this more or less applies to the whole act. He is a celluloid hero, an empty cipher conforming to the "tough guy" image which people want to see in their young men. This popular image can never be real because it is incompatible with the hero's other qualities.

Dick O'Riley, the Communist agitator, and Willie Savard, the employer, are both "real" lumberjack types. They are strong and unruly. Their struggle is brief and violent, and if they dress up their arguments in order to sway the men, they have no illusions themselves. All of this makes an effective contrast for Pierre Boisjoly. Pierre wants to be great and virtuous, that is to embody the whole *rayonnement* ideal. Denis Boucher has already told him that this is impossible, a view which the author seems to share. His desire to wage war on society finds a vague idealistic expression, but crumbles at the approach of real problems carrying real responsibility; he is haunted by fear of guilt as well as obsessed by dreams of grandeur.

Dick, the Communist, pricks the bubble of Pierre's idealism, the idealism of a favourite Quebec way of thinking. The idea of a specially gifted people being a bastion of spiritual values is commonly linked with the paternalistic family business. Dick demonstrates that business, the kind of "materialism" that paternalism is supposed to keep out, is the real victor within the capitalist system:

J'ai appris qu'une foule de petits capitalistes dans votre genre, qui jouent depuis des années la comédie du sentiment, font croire à leurs employés qu'ils font partie d'une famille dont ils sont les fils fidèles. Seulement le patron garde tout, et le bilan truqué qui démontre au fisc une perte, lui sert en même temps à dire à ses employés: "Vous voyez, je perds de l'argent, je me ruine à cause de vos bons gages." Vous leur dansez une gigue, vous parlez de l'ancien temps, vous pleurez un peu et le tour est joué. Mais vous continuez à faire des affaires.[12]

Pierre, seminarist and would-be champion of the people, has no answer, even though he has just won a tactical advantage.

When Pierre's apparent victory is shown to be another mere illusion, the episode is over. As lumber camp hero he has been completely deflated, and will go on to be deflated in other heroic postures. The lumber camp itself, finally, is not quite what it ought to be. Willie Savard, the pious, paternalistic boss, is as socially unacceptable as his *coureur de bois* ancestors. As for Dick, the bold liberator of the French-Canadian people, he is of Irish extraction and Russian training. The noble ideals of traditionalism and popular resistance have both come tumbling down like clowns at a circus.

Several novels show a man close to nature as a bringer of healthy vitality. Agaguk's sexual feats are a blatant example. Hermann, of Yves Thériault's *Le Dompteur d'ours*, is another fairly clear case. By the time he leaves the village, his message has brought a healthy relief to all whose lives had become cramped, embittered or joyless. Hermann is ultimately a "hard savage" type: he wanders at his will, is strong and attractive to women, and his identification with the bears he claims to fight makes him effectively into a man of the forest, although he eventually proves to be a fraud. Germaine Guèvremont's *Le Survenant* offers a particularly striking example, because it is

[12]Roger Lemelin, *Pierre le magnifique* (Paris: Flammarion, 1953), 95.

119

essentially a regionalist novel. The farm life shown through the Beauchemin family is dying, and the breath of life it needs comes from the aimless wanderer. He too is strong, attractive to women and in some way superior to the villagers. His skill at hunting and forest lore supplement his irresponsibility as links with the *voyageur* legend; a more concrete vestige of the folk type is his ability to build a canoe.

Le Dompteur d'ours springs ultimately from a moral principle. It shows a group of people in a village, which is a simplified way of posing the problem of living in society. They have accepted a moral code, yet the spirit of emancipation is necessary. The lives of the different characters revealed in the course of the narrative have one thing in common. They are cramped by the pressures of habit or public opinion. Escape being offered in the form of the bear fighter, they all undergo a crisis. Hermann himself is eventually to disappear without actually fighting the bear they provide. Yet his effect is in each case real. The spirit of emancipation, even of licence, has entered those who suffer from constraint. Dissatisfied women have dared to imagine running away with him, angry parents have reconsidered the problems of youth, youth has made its various gestures of independence. The episodes, jointly and individually, culminate in a new vigour for facing the human lot, a vigour derived from the will to escape brought by the pseudo-savage.

The same therapeutic association has been observed in English-Canadian novels. Hugh MacLennan's *The Watch that Ends the Night* deals mainly with Jerome Martell, a Montreal surgeon. Martell is the bringer of life, both personally and professionally. His only memories of childhood take him to a forest up a lonely river, and to the brutal vitality on which he was nurtured there. In *Sick Heart River*, John Buchan describes the therapeutic journey of a French-Canadian financier. His health can only be renewed by returning to the *pays d'en haut* without plans or any other sop to his organized life in New York. In the Far North an enclave of vitality is discovered on a river which is half real and half dream. This is the simplest expression of the magic which the man of nature finds in the *pays d'en haut*.

Yves Thériault's Agaguk and Ashini together form the most interesting new development historically. They are respectively an

Eskimo and a Montagnais Indian whose characters are drawn from the author's observations in Ungava. Like the early missionaries, Thériault has made his observations in the light of an existing tradition. The result is in some ways a renewal of the whole noble savage process. Yet in Agaguk there is also a definite *coureur de bois* coefficient. Agaguk is the man who has left the village and chosen to live in his own way outside its jurisdiction. Yves Thériault warns his reader that the society depicted is not of the Eskimos as they are, but as they used to be. This device both recalls the element of distance which has always been necessary to happy savage stories and creates a fictitious world in which the forces of *rayonnement* and personal liberty are dramatized together.

It would be an understatement to say that Agaguk is free, since the whole of the action involves the dual struggle for freedom, that of the village, and that of the individual. The action, too, shows him to be noble and good. It is not his fault that he sometimes goes wrong: each crime is the direct reaction to a swindling trader's frustrating Agaguk's worthy plans. Like Joseph-Charles Taché's Père Michel, he kills an unjust man and pays the full price in a long struggle with his conscience. The outcome of the struggle is the emancipation of his wife, and a break with the custom of infanticide.

The struggle itself is not a conscious one, since Agaguk and Iriook are ignorant of morals. All they have learned from the priest is to drink tea. Their own natural goodness is unconscious and unreasoned, which probably explains why it is so drastically upset by outside interference in the form of the whisky trader. Their conscious knowledge is of nature, mainly through the medium of hunting. The struggle is therefore set in Agaguk's contact with nature. He is hunted by a strange white wolf.

The boundary between internal and external nature is completely abolished as the struggle goes on. Agaguk has always been aware of the threat of wolves in the ordinary way, especially when he has accumulated too much meat. But the prize in this contest is the new man. Firstly, Agaguk becomes convinced that the real prey of the white wolf is his son, in whom are vested his vague hopes for the future and the better life he is building. Finally, he wins the struggle when his face has been mauled enough to destroy his original identity, the unregenerate man. This accident saves him from being arrested for murder, but at the same time completes his break with the corrupt village and certain Eskimo traditions. Not only is Agaguk a noble savage, he has also been reborn into a purer state. The struggle with the white wolf is greater, for him, than the break with custom, and a more decisive step in his regeneration. It represents the growth of conscience which must accompany his increased prosperity and ambition. Because Yves Thériault realizes that moral simplicity or neutrality is not enough, he shows a hero transformed by the responsibility of a man who wants to do the right things in a world full of wrong.

An essential of this state is vitality, which Agaguk has in the form of virility and hunting prowess, underlined by Thériault's insistence on sexual activity, in blunt, short sentences. It is the vitality of nature. When Agaguk exults in his wife's pregnancy, he thinks about teaching his son to hunt, and in his dream lesson the whole predatory chain of Ungava's wild life is reconstructed, with victorious man precariously successful in it.

. . . Viens, viens avec moi jusqu'à ces herbes. Ici la piste du vison, regarde! Elle se confond avec celle du rat musqué. Bon, avance et regarde, là! Du sang, du poil. Un rat musqué est mort, dévoré par le vison. Pour eux aussi, l'un comme l'autre, la rançon de la survie. Pour que le vison vive, le rat musqué est sacrifié.

. . . .

Mais il n'y avait pas que les bêtes. Il y avait aussi les armes. Ceci est un fusil . . . Examine comment il est fait. Voici le canon par où surgit la balle d'acier. Ici l'âme de ce canon. Et la crosse. Voici comment il faut charger l'arme. Comment il faut l'épauler, tirer. Vois là-bas ce caribou qui fuit . . . Je presse ici, la balle jaillit, va frapper l'animal.

. . . .

Il lui dirait tout cela à ce petit qu'il aurait. Chaque jour il lui enseignerait les mystères de leur propre survie accordée à celle des animaux de la toundra.[13]

Vitality gives Agaguk the ability to make progress, which the village Eskimos lacked. The point is not that Yves Thériault has left a careless contradiction in his picture of Eskimos; judged as sociology, *Agaguk* would not go very far in spite of its trappings

[13]Yves Thériault, *Agaguk* (Quebec: Institut littéraire, 1958), 52–53.

of language and custom. This apparent inconsistency is a novel way of endowing natural man with perfectibility instead of perfection. His wife, Iriook, represents the emancipation of Eskimo women. References to Eskimo women who are more submissive to tradition suggest a lack of any recognizable human dignity. Iriook's emancipation is distinctly expressed by her giving advice to Agaguk, by speaking up for him in front of the police and in general by participating constructively in their day to day life. It is also shown by untraditional sexual liberties, by insisting on saving the life of a female baby, and generally by being on the side of life in the most elementary ways. Iriook is not wholeheartedly supported by Agaguk, but she wins because in her maternity she holds the life-giving force. She completes Agaguk's break with the obnoxious sexual customs of the village. These, whatever their foundation in the Arctic past, have become corrupt, and support the tyranny of the aging chief and his sorcerer lieutenant. Agaguk wins, not because he is less guilty, but because he is less decadent. In fact, it is Agaguk's crime which leads to the collective fall of the village, and his own disfigurement. Under the influence of his wife, Agaguk is able to begin thinking of himself as a free moral agent, a better being than the one who impulsively killed a swindler. From this he is able to see his past act as a crime, and develops from his remorse the first awareness of conscience. For Thériault, aimless personal freedom and natural vitality are the first sources of moral dignity. He has given this idea a novel if at times highly spiced expression, and developed one more meaning from the myth of the *pays d'en haut*.

Agaguk and Iriook make this moral progress in defiance of sorcerer and chief. Their village represents societies where church and state conspire against individual freedom. They refuse to participate in its decadent customs and to share its fate. For French Canadians of the Duplessis era the use of national solidarity as a battle cry to mask corruption and stifle opposition was a live question. It is no surprise that Yves Thériault should have gone to northern settings for their traditional anti-conformism, and to the happy savage for the equation of freedom with moral good. What is strikingly original is the way in which so many of the main *pays d'en haut* themes have been brought together: the noble savage, his special variant in the *coureur de bois* type, the mystic ordeal with nature (admittedly in this case not a journey) and *rayonnement*, including both cultural conflict and a saved savage. This must account for a great part of the force and consequent popularity of *Agaguk*.

In *Poussière sur la ville*, André Langevin carries the theme of essential freedom to an ultimate conclusion. His Madeleine assumes completely the characteristics of the *libertin*, for she recognizes no law. Her character is the logical projection of the "hard savage" looking for happiness in human nature. She is doomed to death from the start, and seems a hypothetical character in that it is hard to see how she could ever have lived long enough for the action of the novel to take place. Nevertheless, *Poussière sur la ville* is a normal realistic novel, with characters, setting and verisimilitude. Descriptions of scenery have symbolic value without losing their natural basis.

Revolt against society is the obvious first step in Madeleine's search for happiness. She starts by contravening its rule of decorum, and, faced with the alternatives of giving in or going further, she commits adultery, attempted murder, and suicide. The author insists on the solidarity of Macklin, on its narrowness, shallowness and on the tryranny of public opinion over the individual. Against this tyranny, and in view of the way she is forced by gossip to take steps which she might otherwise not have taken, Madeleine appears to have an innocence not unlike that of Louise Genest or Agaguk.

Madeleine's desire for freedom goes far beyond rejecting the canons of her society. She also wants to be free from practical limitations. She never thinks of the financial consequences of her behaviour, any more than of the risk of getting wet if she goes out in the rain. "Une imprudence lui coûte peu," observes her husband.[14] Elsewhere he compares her improvidence to that of a wild animal. He might have thought of happy savages. This absolute disregard for consequences is the antithesis of the calculating civic men of Macklin. Her own greatest moral shock is the discovery that her lover does not really care for her enough to resist social pressures.

Anti-social, innocent, improvident and naturally free from

[14]André Langevin, *Poussière sur la ville*, 2nd ed. (Paris: Laffont, 1955), 177.

124

bonds such as matrimony, Madeleine is essentially of the same family as the characters discussed so far. However, she departs from the tradition through being unable to accept the bonds of her own natural impulses. It is particularly evident that she will not accept the pact which is implicit in her love for her husband. From disdaining the conventional language of love to the more tangible incidents of her adultery, she never ceases to love him, and never begins to consider him. He analyses:

Oh! non, je ne lui passerai pas le licol! C'est en liberté qu'il me faut la posséder. . . . L'appareil de la loi n'est pas pour l'intimider. De droits sur elle, je n'ai que ceux qu'elle accepte. Un pacte pour la vie? Madeleine ne signe pas de pactes, ne se donne pas en contrat. . . . Elle se moquerait la première du mot communion et de tous les autres qui suggèrent l'image de deux amants unis en un seul. [P. 64]

The entire novel, both in action and in comment, indicates that the freedom sought by Madeleine is absolute. This is why she cannot even accept the engagements of her own nature, in the way that a lover like Thomas Clarey can. Her freedom is "une liberté quasi animale" (p. 17) and not easily compatible with even a society of two persons. She is torn with grief on discovering that her affair inevitably hurts her husband. The author is aware, but she is evidently not, that it is simply not possible to do all the things that she wants to do without stumbling on some such inevitable limitation. He makes the husband comment: "Madeleine était si belle qu'elle ne pouvait continuer d'aller ainsi en liberté. Elle appelait la destruction" (p. 146). Consequently, her eventual suicide merely ratifies what we have known all through the novel: a person like Madeleine cannot exist in reality. She has tried to be free of reality: "elle ne s'est pas avouée vaincue parce qu'elle n'a pas trouvé l'absolu avec moi" (p. 153), "elle forcera la réalité à épouser son rêve" (p. 176). Her suicide is the only act which fits logically with such a boundless need for freedom: "Elle s'est donné la liberté définitive" (p. 193).

The husband's position is analogous to that of the civilized man who looks to nature as the source of vitality, goodness and such happiness as he can find. His wild horse simile echoes the famous peroration of Rousseau's *Second Discourse*. After Madeleine's departure he comments that the dusty air of the town he lives in is becoming unbreathable, as he had earlier observed that in losing her he was losing the best part of himself. That is exactly what Madeleine really stands for: the part of a man that is lost when he gives in, the part of a man that goes on living illogically when we have become aware of our limitations, the part of a man that cannot rest within those limitations. Madeleine is like the natural man within us, and when he defends her, Alain defends humanity. His defence of absolute freedom is based on a belief in human nature which is largely identified with Madeleine.

—Elle refuse son devoir parce qu'elle s'y croit supérieure. Elle ne respecte que son intérêt.

—Lui avez-vous dit tout cela?

—Oui, et elle ne m'a même pas écouté. Elle m'a éconduit sans en avoir l'air.

. . . .

—Vous ne pouvez tolérer un être libre autour de vous. J'ai dit cela sans méchanceté. Une constatation froide.

—Personne n'est libre de scandaliser. La liberté ne consiste pas à se soustraire aux lois naturelles et divines.

—Pour moi, la liberté c'est de pouvoir se rendre au bout de son bonheur.

—Je ne vous entends pas.

—Le bonheur d'un être est plus précieux que votre indignation.

Le curé tourne sa grosse figure vers moi. Il est piqué. Il ne prévoyait sans doute pas ma réaction.

—A ce compte-là, vous justifieriez le meurtre par le bonheur que l'assassin en retire.

—Je ne crois pas que le meurtre rende heureux. [P. 161]

Yet nature does not make Madeleine happy, and there is no possibility of her being satisfied within the natural limits of the human condition. In trying to make the people of Macklin love her, Alain has taken on the endless task of making men accept their freedom, which appears to be the only source of dignity, love, pity and such other qualities as humans accept as the nearest thing to happiness.

Despite major changes, there are vestiges of the traditional literary type. The most evident is in the appearance of Richard Hétu, the lover: "—ce garçon fait pour couper des arbres en forêt . . . sa nature primitive, son caractère de bon sauvage" (p. 175). Although he turns out to be a sham, Madeleine sees him as a heroic type like one of DesRochers's lumberjacks. His failure to be what he appears and what Madeleine sees in him is exactly parallel to Macklin's failure to be the joyous freedom which ought to be found in the *pays d'en haut*. Macklin's inhuman landscape as well as its imaginary location among the asbestos mines of the Eastern Townships relate it firmly to the *pays d'en haut* tradition. Its isolation, danger and wonder are the same as René Chopin's "Paysages polaires," although their entry into the theme of the novel is completely different from his aesthetic pose. The traveller through it has the adventurousness of a *voyageur*, even in a car:

Le centre de la route est très glissant, mais, vers son accotement, la neige forme une corrugation où les pneus mordent bien. De me promener seul ainsi la nuit dans un paysage enneigé me donne toujours une étrange impression, celle de traverser un pays mort, dévasté par quelque catalysme extraordinaire. La lueur bleue de la neige reste comme une menace, une irradiation mortelle. [P. 114]

The hero is like the missionaries of the *rayonnement* legend, a traveller bearing a vital message associated with the birth of a child. It is of course a different message, as he will have to kill the child, but there can be no doubt that however different the answer, he is facing the same question. This is frontier country, entering the theme of the novel to denote a spiritual frontier.

These distinct vestiges, especially when considered in the light of Langevin's other works, show that *Poussière sur la ville* is still close to the *pays d'en haut* tradition. Madeleine's relation to the lineage of the *coureur de bois* is slight but essential. Langevin has reduced the local colour that went with *Louise Genest* to a few images and significant descriptions. But these images and descriptions amount to a fairly systematic occurrence, providing the link between theme, character and setting. They give the novel its artistic unity.

The libertine character in French-Canadian literature has so often been associated with *pays d'en haut* figures that it is possible to conclude that this is a distinct internal development. Its latest manifestations have clearly absorbed much modern French influence, but are also a recognizable outcome of tendencies which can be traced back to older influences in Canada. From what we know of attitudes and reactions common among the early settlers, it may be said that, even in the absence of a direct literary continuity, there is some kind of continuity from those days to the present time. It is discerned mainly in a persistent dream of freedom in the forest.

In literature that can be called French-Canadian, the main developments of the libertine type have been first an increase in local colour relating him to French-Canadian social types, and then a falling away of that local colour as he becomes more a vehicle for developing an author's own preoccupations. A part of the first tendency was a fusion of the savage types which Lovejoy, Boas, *et al.* call "hard" and "soft," the latter being vested in a conformist man suitable for *survivance* propaganda. In the second tendency that fusion dissolved, and there was a return to an increasingly "hard" savage, in whom local colour, though continuing to have considerable importance (as with Bertrand Vac) is more than balanced by an exploration of the relations between freedom and happiness or moral perfection. One recent development (notably with Yves Thériault) is a return from French-Canadian to aboriginal local colour, with a corresponding increase in the theoretical breadth of the argument. Another striking development is the almost complete elimination of local colour, so that Langevin's Madeleine is, superficially, barely recognizable as part of the tradition. She is an almost purely theoretical embodiment of the libertine hypothesis that what man seeks is happiness.

Madeleine is none the less a logical conclusion for the whole theme, and it is she who most completely rediscovers the dilemma which Frenchmen like Sagard found in the first impact of arrival in Canada. Aloof from French Catholic morals, she pursues her happiness to the very end without question. This gives her a purity through which, like Sagard's polyandrous Hurons, she is somehow superior to the sordid money-grubbers who claim the right to extend their civilization even into her life. Dubois feels that her example can somehow raise the spiritual level of those people, in the same way as it raised a revolt in him. He is the missionary converted by the children of nature, the civilized man who finds himself on a spiritual and geographical frontier. Langevin's creation is therefore not simply an application of the "live dangerously" formula, it is the awareness of a Frenchman who wakes up after three centuries to find that he is still in Canada.

CHAPTER SIX

Revolt

It follows from the foregoing chapters that in all the French-Canadian literature which recalls the spirit of the old *pays d'en haut* there is some element of escape, usually from social or intellectual conformity. Ironic literature, making fun of the ideals of French-Canadian history and social leadership, refutes the attempt to draw the *pays d'en haut* into nationalist conformity. Criticism of a narrow provincial outlook sometimes turns to a strong feeling against society in general. In this case, characters derived from the *coureur de bois* type are no longer simply escaping, but lead the social revolt into something more like a reaction to the human condition common among modern French writers. The influence of Camus is noticeable but the writer's imagination is still clearly stimulated by the *pays d'en haut*, which are an authentic French-Canadian source of rebel feelings.

The geographical facts of the *pays d'en haut* make them into an obvious symbol for escape. Journeys into the pseudo-North like those of Ringuet's *Fausse monnaie* combine a literal with figurative levels of escape in a way that seems quite natural. The historic function of the *coureur de bois* provides a corresponding literary type of man. It presents the side of man which is not responsive to measurable co-ordinates. The attempt to find the whole man leads to a world remote from customary divisions. The human figure and the scenery are the elements of a world nostalgically associated with the historic *pays d'en haut*, with vital moral conflict, with untamed nature, with the memory of past adventures and the yearning for a long search.

For many French-Canadian writers this utopia in the North is a complete imaginative setting for their most searching questions, while for others it is a myth which provokes irony. While this double function is the consequence of a truth general to all literary myths, it has some special causes in Canada. The ironic revolt will be illustrated here by Ringuet's *Un Monde était leur empire* and *Fausse monnaie*. An opposition to French-Canadian moral values, close to but more direct than ironic reaction, will be considered in Yves Thériault's *Cul-de-sac*. Gabrielle Roy's *Alexandre Chenevert* will be further considered as a wider challenge to social and religious values, and André Langevin's *Le Temps des hommes* will be examined, with necessary reference to his *Poussière sur la ville*, as the best example of a "Northern" theme in metaphysical revolt.

Rayonnement, in the first place an expression of escape from an alien domination, has associated the imagined *pays d'en haut* with an authoritarian national outlook. This may be considered as a kind of escape, drawing on the boundless vitality of Northern themes. Its limitation is that most of the time it is too obviously sublimated politics. Lacking spontaneity and sincerity, it has not created a myth so much as a manifesto. *Sources* is a case in point, precisely because Desrosiers appears to avoid the pitfall of living in a history that never took place. Despite its ingenious practical arguments, despite even the fact that the solution it offers is practicable on a small scale, the novel is an escape from historical realities. The future it offers is a thing of the past. The growth and development it recommends are a disguised refusal of change. Despite its superficial appeal and a great deal of dedication on the part of its writers, *rayonnement* has not made such good literature out of the North as the rebel spirit has. Between the argument and the inspiration there is an historic contradiction, and the large amount of *rayonnement* literature attests mainly to the appeal of the northern scene to writers in search of vigour.

Un Monde était leur empire is the ironic final product of the whole *rayonnement* tradition, which it never directly mentions. Ringuet, in his Preface, makes his intention clear. He wants to think of Canadians as part of an American continent with its own history and character. He will use history to correct the false perspective which makes the American peoples, and especially French Canadians, think of themselves primarily by reference to their European heritage.

The major phases of Ringuet's history are like a *roman à clé* within the French-Canadian literary tradition. The evocation of anonymous nomads crossing the Bering Strait without harangue is an antithesis to the cherished pictures of French explorers planting cross and flag. Ville-Marie and the other two centres are not even named, but obviously intended in a contemptuous reference to "quelques misérables hameaux étrangers."[1] The structure of the book is the most eloquent rejection of a tradition which has always made French endeavour the main part of American history. Part I deals with the pre-Columbian period. It has 209 pages, of which a mere eleven are devoted to Europeans before Columbus, and another ten to geological history. Part II has 120 pages, going from official European discovery to the present day. About one third of this looks over the present situation and presents an argument. The events which are normally thought of as American history are confined to one short chapter, since most of the author's interest in the occupation of the continent is to study its effect on the existing civilizations. The prominence given to Maya and Inca civilizations is a plain rejection of the myth of a French civilizing mission. Some of the minor "Indian" societies are more important than any one European establishment. There is an evident flaw in the arrangement. Ringuet has still had to make Columbus into the pivot of his continental history, even while denying his importance. The thing rejected is the real point of the book, and things not mentioned are its subject.

The Leif Eiriksson episode is a fair example of how Ringuet uses genuine history, and no doubt genuinely neglected history, to break the accepted idols of the past. In the first place he relates it in such a way as to create a sympathy for "Indians" versus European invaders. In the second place he uses these same Europeans to counter the prestige of those whose exploits have been better recorded and with more flattery as well. The Norse explorers were men exiled from their own country for murder. The first thing they did was to murder a few of the American natives. They are referred to as "civilisés" with quotation marks. The later revenge of the natives is viewed with sympathy. A setting is evoked which adds to the feeling that a few brutes came

[1]Philippe Panneton (pseud. Ringuet), *Un Monde était leur empire* (Montreal: Editions Variétés, 1943), 504.

to disturb a golden harmony with a bountiful nature. Yet, if the right of first occupation goes indisputably to the peoples whose ancestors had entered via the Bering Straits, the second prize is for these first European individuals. The Norsemen were the first to settle in the Gulf of St. Lawrence, the first to witness the birth of their own children on this continent. By implied comparison with the later searchers for gold, they become innocent brutes, looking for a more hospitable land than Greenland and failing to settle in peace through an error rather than a wicked ambition.

The French part in American history is reduced to mere mentions in a general chapter on endeavours secondary to those of Spain and Portugal. In total, nevertheless, they are the main part of that chapter, which shows where Ringuet's main iconoclastic intention lies. The religious motive is not discussed, but France is patently grouped with the heretic nations which had no regard for the papal bull dividing the New World. The missionary martyrs are damned with faint praise in a context showing that the main gifts of the white man were brandy and fire-arms. While Ringuet avoids obvious Happy Savage themes, a few tinted remarks like, "le sauvage pourra vivre librement sa vie," still escape him (p. 304). If the cruelty of the Indians to each other is mentioned, it is only to point out that the great Champlain made, quite by accident, the mistake of an alliance with the losing side. Ultimately, this event led to the fall of French power in America, as well as to the biassed notion that the Hurons were innocent victims of incomparably savage Iroquois.

Un Monde était leur empire is not the best history of the continent, but as a purge for constipated myths it is without compare. Ringuet has not only rejected the cherished picture of a nation of priests, he has also upset the more real and less deliberate creation, a nation of historians. There is, however, one part of the main myth which he has not rejected. He is still looking to the *pays d'en haut* for truth, destiny, peace and freedom, and an escape from established doctrines.

This type of irony throws added light on *Trente Arpents*, which is an undisputed landmark among French-Canadian novels. The same kind of insistent omission is here applied to the pioneering side of the *rayonnement* myth. Father Labelle, an historical figure in settling the Laurentian North, is mentioned by name. Euchariste Moisan's childhood memories speak of the material failure of planned pioneering. They also create a moral environment, whose failure is evident in his hard character and total lack of feeling for his deceased parents.

Euchariste's three principal sons continue the same theme among others. They represent three French-Canadian historical types: the priest, the peasant and the deserter. Oguinase fulfils his father's destiny by dying of privations in a new colony. Etienne maintains the narrowness of the eternal family land and the character of its dependants. Ephrem, the most admired son, inherits the adventurous spirit which leads him to settle in New England. He is a fine example of what the province has to offer its own cherished sons. His "desertion" to another life in another country is inevitable, because his own society has no place for him.

Fausse monnaie, slighter and simpler than Ringuet's best known work, shows a more developed and more delicate irony. This does not merely occur in passing, but is the substance of the work. However, it shows the same restraint from buffoonery and from bitterness, and gives the novel an elegant, lucid construction. This takes the form of a journey very similar to the magic journeys discussed in Chapter Four. There is a reluctant departure from Montreal by car, by a group of young people whose sentimental relations with each other demonstrate some six types of amorous couple. They contemplate the scenic beauty of the Montrealers' week-end "North" and undergo parallel experiences. After hesitations and restraints there is for the principal characters a first escape, in the moonlight, to sweet memories of childhood. Later, the whole party walks up a mountain, and the characteristically irregular climb is accompanied by the development of their erotic interest, mostly in discreet or vague terms, so that the possibility of ironic doubt is prepared in the mind of the reader. André and Suzanne reach an ideal summit gazing at the Laurentian scenery and the sky, and withdrawn into an intimate imaginary garden. There is a hurried and disorderly descent, in which lingering regret is mingled with disillusion and bad weather. A last part emphasizes their complete return to the characters they thought they had left behind. This completes the doubt we had of the reality of the elevating experience.

The perfect coincidence of the erotic journey with the paradigm of the ideal journey lends an unobtrusive force to the whole ironic conception of the novel. As the characters approach their ideal, they are rejecting the values on which their everyday life is based. When their failure becomes evident, the nature of the ideal itself is called into question. The final ambiguity leaves no doubt that, of their everyday life and their moral elevation, one or both must be false.

The first movement is an escape towards purity and nature. From a Montreal of mundane pleasures, the characters travel to a landscape which is purified of commercial civilization; André above all finds a purer self. External nature and a lofty kind of human nature come together. All the members of the party find an inner response to a sudden scene of beauty. External nature is linked with their state of mind, as it expands into visions of forest, mountain and vast skies. In their picnic, the climbers are all liberated from their tawdry jobs in the city, to become gay and childlike again. Like Alexandre Chenevert, they may be prisoners in a sordid materialistic society, but they have a way of escape. The vulgarity of their life can be observed by this device, and they will finally return to it.

From the very beginning this change is equivocal. It is shown mainly through the understanding which is reached between André and Suzanne. But this intelligence may have arisen only from caprices of timing and misunderstanding. At the very moment that their handclasp feels like the imprint of eternity, Ringuet is without comment anticipating the brevity of their tenderness. Even when they seem supremely detached from their old selves and have recognized their failure to understand each other, André has nothing to say to Suzanne. As her aloofness breaks down, and his shallow pleasure-hunting is discarded, they reach the sublime state of having exchanged rôles. It is ironically inappropriate, for they are not really meeting even when each feels able to enter the other's world. Their descent from such illumination is marked by petty details. The first is that Suzanne feels cold, and André's gesture of offering his jacket is halted by the thought that he might catch a chill from the evening breeze. A series of similar small gestures shows each couple coming down to earth from whatever heights they had attained. There is an intermediate culmination in which they all seem rather bad-tempered because they are hungry.

What looked like such charming or even noble affections are reduced to sentimental illusions. With them is reduced the arch illusion of the purity of nature in the stirring North. Before the novel ends, André has returned to his preference for facile pleasures without conviction, and Suzanne to her snobbish pretensions without feeling. It is never certain whether Ringuet was more satirical about what they had returned to or about the belief that they could ever have escaped. Thus, he is sceptical of both the society and the myth.

Cul-de-sac, as its title indicates, is mainly concerned with the problem of escape. Freedom is no longer good without complication, as it was in Yves Thériault's earlier novels. The positive good is to be found in love, and personal freedom is an essential prerequisite, capable of extending from good to evil. It is characterized by reference to a restrictive society, so that inevitably there is a certain amount of social protest. However, *Cul-de-sac* is not simply a satire; the inner struggle remains and destroys its hero even after the immediate restrictions of society have been removed. His choice is not between a good nature and a corrupt society.

Victor Debreux's picture of provincial society is none the less integral to his escape. The figure of his father, seconded by that of his employer, amounts to a stifling patriarchy. Its virtues are self-interest, respectability and polished hypocrisy; its vices are scandal, art and social heresy. Yves Thériault obviously felt under no obligation to develop these points at length in 1961, because this is already an accepted way of dealing with French-Canadian society in French-Canadian novels.

Debreux's empty existence is controlled by the collective "we" of family and friends, or by economic and similar circumstances. His employer and his father are both successful men, whose every action, word and gesture is calculated and controlled. Both work and pleasure are dictated to the young man, who follows like a sheep even to the extent of having a fiancée incorporated into his weekly habits without having felt any interest in her. His idea of freedom was that of his ambient culture:

La liberté, cela signifiait l'occasion de commettre le mal à l'insu de ses parents. Le devoir des parents étant de protéger leurs enfants contre le péché, et le péché de l'impureté étant . . . *quod erat.* . . . On n'en sortait pas.

Il ne devrait pas être nécessaire de le dire. Nous sommes les produits de cet âge et nous ne savons plus trop bien comment en sortir. Le danger, me disait un directeur de conscience, en première philo, c'est de se sentir pris au piège, de faire un effort terrible pour se dégager, et que cet effort, mal calculé, nous libère en effet, mais nous projette tête première dans l'abîme.

(Debreux has in fact literally fallen into an abyss at the time of recalling all this).

Sa conclusion était simple: par prudence, rester dans le piège. (Je lui avais demandé conseil sur la sensation d'étouffement que me procurait l'étude de Saint Thomas dans le manuel imposé.)[2]

Debreux was the perfect passive creature desired by the authoritarians, and imprisoned in their plan for French-Canadian manhood.

By the device of having his hero recall his life story while awaiting death in a stark granite crevice, the author is able to transpose upon that society its culmination in a physical and figurative prison. His is a history of wandering that has led only from one kind of prison to another. The helpless victim is being eaten by a hawk while recalling how his days were consumed in a fruitless search. The story of Montreal society has been transposed into an Ungava setting, which gives it a new perspective. The northern countryside adds a meaning; it gives a spiritual dimension to what might otherwise be a purely social problem:

J'ai aimé ce pays chaque fois que j'y suis venu.

Je l'ai aimé parce qu'il savait je ne sais trop comment ni pourquoi me combler, m'emplir l'âme. Il me rassurait. Ici, mon vide était parfois moins vide, et ce qui en restait alors rendait des échos bizarrement tendres. [P. 54]

Debreux is an engineer, and he is a man caught in a trap of raw granite. It is in the symbolic suggestions of these two sides of the central character that the meaning of the novel is most evident. As an engineer he has been trained to submit everything to measurements. He frequently mentions mathematical tables

[2]Yves Thériault, *Cul-de-sac* (Quebec: Institut littéraire, 1961), 32.

with a metaphorical sense for measuring human values and he challenges the reader to work out the *cote morale* of his love affair as if challenging the worth of their measuring instruments. Another aspect of his profession is controlling the forces of nature in forms such as dams. As a trapped man he thinks of the futility of measurements or controls, and looks back on love and life as something to be wallowed in: instead of control he looks for spontaneity. Through love properly understood, he would have lived with nature and man; this is mainly what is meant by introducing a passage from Teilhard de Chardin.

Four ways of escape are present in the total narrative: drink, work, love, and death. Drink is a false escape which lands young Debreux in a dipsomaniac clinic, still under the supervision of his family. Finally it leads him into his fatal predicament in Ungava. Still, it is an initial escape. In the beginning Debreux feels grateful to an alcoholic stranger who made him see his own futility so clearly. Their meeting brings in the first reference to rebirth, introducing the theme of spiritual regeneration. The stranger's finger, with which he prods Debreux while telling him of his inner void, is like an umbilical cord. Debreux does escape to the extent of realizing that the word "pareil" is an accusation, not an approbation. This is his first chance to become himself. The second drinking crisis is regarded with more indulgence, because it is an escape from sudden grief. This is a feeble echo of its first potentiality. The last reference to drink (apart from the very end of the book) shows a complete debasement of this kind of freedom: he is free to be drunk because he is underpaid by his last employer.

A more effective escape is hard work. This is more toxic than drink, because it absorbs his lucidity, gives him peace with society, and so takes his mind off his real problem. This kind of activity could be called "escapism." Pascal's comments[3] on how *divertissement* blinds us to the tragedy of man are recalled by the alcoholic's explanation of the human condition:

—Lorsqu'on craint le vide, on se tient loin des bords. Mais loin des bords, c'est le désert. Et le désert est plat, le désert est sans fin,

---

[3]Blaise Pascal, *Pensées* 205 (Br. 739, 210 . . .), *Œuvres* (Paris: Gallimard, 1962, coll. Pléiade no. 34), 1138 *et seq.*

le désert est mort. La mort de nous, la mort du désert. Nous sommes donc une partie du désert tu vois? Par peur de l'abîme. Et la peur de l'abîme, c'est la peur du vide. Si l'on s'arrête un seul instant, si l'on se détache du quotidien pour regarder au-dedans de soi, on trouve le vide. Un vide qui donne le vertige. . . . [P. 75]

Debreux had always suffered from lack of purpose, because as a perfect conformist he had surrendered his will to authority. Work gives an illusion of purpose.

Love is not escapism. It brings a true feeling of responsibility. It was a real release to Debreux and he compares it with grace, because it freed him from his fear of the void and gave him purpose which made him free to act in professional and personal life. A sketchy anecdote demonstrates (with too much evidence of the author's intention) how it released his intellectual energies into constructive channels. Love is identified with healthy vitality. It changes construction into creation, and management into the service of man.

This portion of the novel, abruptly ended by the senseless death of the loved one for the purpose of dramatic effect, is rather insubstantial. The message of love is plain enough, and the qualification that this does not mean fleshless charitable intentions leaves no doubt as to the author's meaning. Yet it lacks conviction, because the characters and actions do not speak for themselves as much as in the rest of the novel. Love is supposed to be full and invigorating, and then completely destroyed by a motoring accident. True, Debreux mentions his attempt to live up to the level of Fabienne after her death. His failure is explained by the weakness which he has always had. He has always been the prisoner of narrowness and mediocrity, and his escape seems to be dashed by fate. It is only in the journey to Ungava that he acquires any lasting freedom to choose his own end.

Failure has led Debreux into the face of certain death, trapped in a hole. The novel opens with a physical and figurative fall. A long mixture of seeking and avoiding has ended with the hero facing his real situation. Before his bare, broken bone he is able to contemplate his impotence beside nature:

Reculeur de granit! J'ai dirigé des chantiers où l'on a bougé des montagnes. . . . Et ce jourd'hui de mort, ce temps de la haine de l'homme envers lui-même, alors qu'il sait jauger brusquement la

véritable étendue de sa faiblesse, je ne savais même plus reculer deux
parois de granit bleu qui m'enserraient et me retenaient stupidement.

Plus de calculs, plus d'invention, plus d'audace.

Pour une fois l'homme, l'homme originel, aux prises avec le
granit. . . .

Démuni, réduit à mon identité originelle, j'étais impuissant contre
la nature. [Pp. 59–60]

There is nothing left but to welcome his tormentor, the giver of
death. He begs the hawk which has been eating him alive to
bring deliverance.

This thorough discovery, this acceptance of ultimate truth, is
one of the main ends of the journey. It has a considerable paradoxical value. In vast space, Debreux has found a narrow prison;
in his enemy he has found his friend; in evasion he has found
truth; in his absolute dejection there is a certain exaltation. At
this point he is hoisted out of his crevice by a helicopter. This is
not only to add a picture of physical elevation. The sequel which
his rescue provides takes him to a Quebec hospital, and there is
the whole feeling of coming down from the *pays d'en haut* to
ordinary men and ordinary problems. Debreux has to become an
ordinary living man again. He is given a mocking last chance of
regeneration through the hospital priest who tells him that he is
in any case dying of liver cancer. He can drink and die quickly,
or abstain and live a little longer. He will be released from the
hospital and, apparently for the first time in his life, obliged to
make a choice in real freedom. Reversing Pascal's famous hypothesis that a man condemned to death could not waste time
playing cards in prison,[4] Debreux plays a game of argument with
the almoner, avoiding the question until the last minute. Yet in
the taxi that takes him from his hospital, he makes his choice with
the rapid lucidity that once made him a great engineer. The
memory of Fabienne tells him of purpose in life, but he is filled
with repugnance at the thought of giving his dead father the
satisfaction of an edifying death. The reader realizes that the story
has come full circle: he is the young man in the bar, and Debreux
is the alcoholic stranger showing him the emptiness of our existence. Despite his own negative end (in effect the refusal of grace,
since that is what Fabienne means to him) Debreux's impending

[4]Pascal, *Pensées* (Br. 61), 1180.

death may have the value of making others assume their freedom more readily than he did.

Alexandre Chenevert, Gabrielle Roy's representative ordinary man, shares this feeling of the paucity of freedom: he reflects that he is free to go to paradise, but not to make any other choice. At the peak of his terrestrial bliss, he wants to share his gift with mankind, but finds that the gift has a limit: he does not know how to communicate it. These are two stages in a long interrogation of God. Alexandre has gone up to the country where man is face to face with God, and found in one experience that there is a limit to man's freedom and God's goodness. Systems have at times been developed to make human limitation more acceptable, but there is something in us which keeps returning to the problem, and rebelling against solutions which offer less freedom than we can imagine. Alexandre Chenevert is an example. His revolt is mild, but it goes to the full extent of his mild character. In spite of its very moderate expression, it is a total revolt.

In this total, neither man nor God will be found adequate. In the central episode, God's goodness is found in external nature. Yet the cruelty of nature is found elsewhere, including the classic example of the death of children. The doctor, whose vocation is to reduce human suffering, has to be willing to work with God's will or against it. He is likely to get lost in the ambiguity of human suffering, but finally it is from his doctor and not from his God that Alexandre receives permission to be happy. Alexandre Chenevert has the special problem of a God in the Jansenist tradition.

Happiness, where it is shown, is an escape from the servitude of time and the mass of obligations, a simple contact with the living experience of the scene. "Eprouver la faim, la contenter" denotes the lost pleasures of civilized man.[5] It is comparable with the way Albert Camus uses North Africans to express the uncomplicated joy he is seeking in *L'Envers et l'endroit* and *Noces*.[6]

The whole story of Chenevert's agitations can be related to three planes: social problems, immediate suffering and specula-

[5]Gabrielle Roy, *Alexandre Chenevert* (Montreal: Beauchemin, 1954), 210.

[6]Cf. John Cruickshank, *Albert Camus and the Literature of Revolt*. 2nd ed. (London: Oxford University Press, 1959), 36.

tive anguish. All of his major worries are real ones in world affairs, and mostly topical at the time the novel was written (e.g. the Palestine problem). They become a pressing reality through being linked medically, either as cause or effect, with his own suffering (as in his insomnia, with which the novel opens). At the same time, the narrative makes a life like his seem a common-place reality. It raises serious questions about human societies and finally must enter into our assessment of the human condi-tion. At times the author makes this multi-planar significance explicit, as when she shows the problem of human misunder-standing extending from the conjugal to the international (p. 114) and ending in a fine stoic silence, or when she confronts Alexandre with the moral problem of income tax.

Ainsi lui-même, en toute honnêté vis-à-vis le Receveur général, était tenu de lui signaler le petit excédent qu'il gagnait ici afin d'arriver à joindre les deux bouts. Il était à peu près sûr que, s'il en avait la possibilité, il éviterait cet excès de franchise. Cependant, c'était tout un problème pour Alexandre que celui du fisc. Quand il songeait à Veuve Honorine Blanche Mathieu, par exemple, il reconnaissait l'injustice qu'il aurait commise en diminuant d'un cent sa part d'impôt qui était peut-être destinée justement à la pauvre vieille. Les hommes ayant manqué de charité, la Loi leur avait dû en faire une stricte obligation. La pénible contrainte représentait donc une sorte de progrès en ce monde.

Cependant, lorsqu'Alexandre pensait que l'on pourrait faire la guerre sans son consentement, dans son dos pour ainsi dire; lorsqu'il pesait et calculait que son petit argent si péniblement gagné pourrait contribuer à tuer quelque inconnu, achèterait des bombes, de ces armes meurtrières dont la seule idée l'empêchait de dormir; alors, au moment d'adresser son chèque au Receveur général, Alexandre se serait souhaité le courage d'aller plutôt en prison. [P. 120]

The term "la condition humaine" is used in the text, denoting a life which is shared between "la gratuité de la misère humaine" (p. 164) and "le goût du bonheur" (p. 179). This is the tragic ambiguity which extends from the real experience of Alexandre's life to the ambiguity which he perceives in God. Baffled by a need to struggle and a sense of futility, he sums up the fresh problems which dog man's efforts: we work to pay for medicines which we need to keep working. To this is added the extra suffering caused by selfishness and dishonesty, such as that encouraged by medical insurance companies. Nevertheless, some faith in human enterprises is necessary, he finds. The novel itself keeps bringing us back to a sense of futility. Extra work found in the evening appears to Alexandre as a kind of freedom, since it helps him to pay off a debt. He does not even see the irony of it. Elsewhere he questions formal declarations of the Rights of Man, but decides he ought to believe in them since sincere people like Mrs. Roosevelt evidently do. The futility of his salutary journey is visible to the reader as soon as the return is begun. In all these gyrations about liberty, health, happiness, Alexandre can never reach a solution, because it is apparently not possible to reconcile man's different needs. When his doctor suggests bowling alleys as a relief to anxieties, the reaction is immediate:

—C'est distrayant, à ce qu'on dit. On jette une boule contre un tas de quilles. Ce n'est pas malin, mais il paraît que cela empêche de penser.

Alexandre le regardait, perplexe, un peu choqué: quoi, se donner tant de peine pour s'empêcher de poursuivre la seule occupation qui compte, la seule raisonnable! [P. 168]

Ultimately, for Alexandre, the tragedy is that it is too hard for man to love God. God bribes us with paradise, but expects love, which Alexandre knows must be totally free. In questioning the justice of God (in whom he never ceases to believe) Alexandre is questioning the seat of all absolutes. Justice, freedom and goodness are all unreliable because God has not made them into the certainties that man needs and seeks to build his world on. The one happy day of Alexandre's life begins with his deliverance from God, man and original sin.

Il descendit un long fleuve d'oubli et lui-même était ce fleuve libre et noir. Il n'avait plus souvenir d'aucune tâche exigée ou interrompue. Il fut délivré de Dieu et des hommes. Alexandre n'avait plus à répondre du péché originel, non plus que de ces armes d'aujourd'hui, si dangereuses qu'on va les essayer en des îles désertes. [P. 203]

But this grace is of short duration. Later, we find him reflecting that prayers always sound mournful, because they must be addressed to someone very harsh.

Even when Alexandre is on the brink of understanding some

higher value in suffering, he realizes that he will no more be able to help men by communicating it than he could when he had discovered the secret of happiness. The argument is completed when the almoner prays for Alexandre's death. Whatever the message of suffering, man is not able to bear it, and God is lacking in the cardinal virtue of charity, since His generosity does not measure up to His power.

Hélas! parce qu'il était Dieu justement, la passion du Christ n'avait pas ému complètement Alexandre. N'y avait-il pas eu des milliers d'hommes qui avaient souffert autant sinon plus que le Christ, pour des motifs dérisoires: des frontières, des histoires d'huile, d'intérêts; parce qu'ils étaient Juifs? Parce qu'ils étaient Japonais? Et combien d'hommes, s'ils avaient eu la possibilité comme Jésus de racheter les autres par leur mort, n'eussent pas longtemps hésité. [P. 318]

Deprived of a set of absolute values which transcend man, Alexandre Chenevert is not able to find in man himself an adequate substitute. During his moment of happiness, he is able to feel grateful towards both man and God. The instant when he feels that men are more to be thanked than God (p. 241) may have lasting significance, but it is not final. The whole episode is like a long balance sheet between man and God. But Alexandre will return to knowing that men do not love each other enough. They cannot reach any important agreement, and they kill each other. They even kill a man like Gandhi, and they feel so little about it that Eugénie can be annoyed by Alexandre's agitation, since after all Gandhi was no relation of theirs. Human justice is only obtained by means of terrible pressures, yet our lack of charity means that we have to have some kind of system. Our understanding of each other is incomplete, and often painful. Even our kind concern can be hurtful. Still, the last action in the novel shows the operation of science in the cause of man, and the last word is that "la seule assurance, sur terre, vient de notre déraisonnable tendresse humaine" (p. 373). Similarly, Alexandre's last satisfaction was the discovery that he had friends, and his last positive action was a movement of sympathy towards another patient.

In hospital, Alexandre is reduced to accepting the world as it is. His last hope is to return to the place he had discovered in the North and be content with it. Fused with this acceptance is an acceptance of man, which even leads to a partial acceptance of God.

Il croyait s'apercevoir qu'il lasserait la patience des autres à trop durer, et il lui était intolérable d'en abuser.

Cependant, cette bonté déconcertante autour de lui ne l'engageait plus à se méfier.

Au contraire, cette bienveillance des autres, c'était ce qui le portait enfin à imaginer Dieu aussi bienveillant . . . si Dieu avait autant de cœur qu'un homme, déjà ce serait beau. . . . [P. 358–9]

Alexandre's final serenity is equivalent, in view of his mild character, to the Absurdist's resignation to a world without deliverance, where human dignity feeds on an inner conquest.

The ethic of revolt does not mean deliverance. It is revolt paradoxically based on acceptance—indignant acceptance of the immutability of the absurd.

. . . .

This perishable immediacy makes the actor's achievement a suitable symbol of life as seen from the absurdist standpoint.

. . . .

[The conqueror] possesses heightened awareness of human potentialities. He is very conscious of "l'étonnante grandeur de l'esprit humain." He stands for the most militant kind of humanism, which combines pride with clarity, and by means of both recognizes the tragic ambivalence of all human creatures.[7]

It would be misleading to place *Alexandre Chenevert* simply under the absurdist label, but its questioning of values is remarkably similar.

André Langevin creates the most extensive and deliberated revolt in French-Canadian literature. It is evident at once in his vocabulary and imagery: "l'inévitable injustice" (T 132), "ses spasmes ébrèchent l'idée d'une justice absolue" (P 48), "refuser avec les hommes" (T 133), "son allié contre l'absurde cruauté" (P 153), and "les bras trop lourds de tourner mon rocher" (P 139) (recalling Albert Camus's revival of the legend of Sisyphus).[8] His plots also denote an anger which is more violent than the

[7]Cruickshank, *Albert Camus*, 74, 79, 83.

[8]Here and in the rest of this chapter, page references to André Langevin's novels will be made by the abbreviations as follows: P = *Poussière sur la ville*, 2nd ed. (Paris: Laffont, 1955); T = *Le Temps des hommes* (Montreal: Le Cercle du Livre de France, 1956).

exploratory revolt of *Alexandre Chenevert* and more absolute than any works of Yves Thériault. The symbolic function of certain recurrent objects, such as the corpses which are prominent in all his novels, puts into relief his thematic use of natural description.

Inevitably, comparison with French writers suggests itself. Assuming that the place of French-Canadian authors within their own tradition has been assessed, how do they compare with other works of the modern revolt? Is it correct or misleading to use the same term for both? Are the Canadian traditions compatible with more recent and more conscious influences from France?

In order to keep the comparison to the main questions, it is necessary to avoid too particular a measurement against individual works, and to start with accepted generalizations. For a clear delineation of these, we are further indebted to John Cruickshank's work on Camus. He shows that the revolt which now dominates the use of that term surpasses the Romantic protest, which was made in the name of a human nature embodying general values. The *lieu commun* to which it may be reduced is "the tragic ambivalence of human existence." The absolute revolt has three main characteristics: moral ambiguity, emphasis on immediate concrete situations rather than abstract attitudes, and human responsibility. To these correspond three levels of significance in an author's narrative: the social, the individual and the speculative, unified by the art of the novelist. At times the metaphysical consideration will arise directly at the literal level, though this is never a sustained allegory. Any conclusion reached will be a paradoxical acceptance rather than a logical necessity. Other signs of revolt are to be found in the texture of a work rather than its ideas. Emphasis on the individual's experience of his physical environment is one of special interest in all *pays d'en haut* literature. The northern forest of *Le Temps des hommes* and the isolated mining town of *Poussière sur la ville* both enter the reader's experience like a direct physical sensation of the world the characters are living in. The direct confrontation of those characters with the universe of depressing landscapes and deadly blizzards is not merely symbolic or metaphorical, though it is also both of these; it is a source of suffering in itself.

145

In *Le Temps des hommes* a journey up to a remote camp is made in difficult conditions in order to open up a new road through a portion of forest. The countryside is charged with ambiguous feelings. The first impressions of peace and clarity give way to an awareness of decay:

—Un maudit pays! constata le cuisinier. . . . Une mort végétale qui coulait goutte à goutte, entassait pourriture sur pourriture, montait de terre avec le sève, atteignait l'air. Même en hiver cela sentait le pourrissement. [T 70]

The ambiguity of external nature is a foreboding of the human drama. The description of decay will be used again after the murder episode is completed. Another ambiguous feature of the forest is the feeling of freedom and space. The men, brought to their final camp by a snowmobile which will not return, feel prisoners. The sky seems lower, the horizon offers no issue. Even Gros Louis, the ideal lumberjack, feels imprisoned in an inhuman country, as soon as he senses that he is cut off from his main camp. Even without consulting the feelings experienced by the characters of the novel, we encounter such expressions as "un espace blanc, morne, lourd . . . le paysage privé d'ombres" (T 9), "le désert planté d'arbres qui s'étendait à l'infini vers le nord" (T 10), and "De trois côtés des collines l'écrasent [Macklin] où on cultive un sol pierreux" (P 26). Langevin clearly intends us to enter his world conceding that, reduced to its elements, it has nothing to offer but a grim struggle. In the last account the landscape is equated with death.

Le vent chassait des tourbillons de neige au-dessus d'eux. Il ferma les yeux et la panique lui étreignit le cœur. Il allait mourir ainsi, allongé à côté de Laurier, mourir de froid, de faim, enseveli sous la neige. La mort était ce grand espace blanc qui se dilatait dans sa tête, . . . [T 229]

This blank, inhuman mass is the stage on which human destinies are played out, but at best nothing more than that. It is a universe in which man has no fixed starting point, an existence which has no form other than that which man will give it.

Metaphor makes further links between the human problem

and the physical universe. Whenever Dubois finds that he is giving in to the tragic emptiness of society or death, he finds he has "l'âme couverte de poussière" (P 120) just as Yolande has "du givre sur l'âme" (T 58), to describe her failure and loneliness. In both novels, the physical universe is being made to work in a moral or emotional sense which is not independent of the direct, obvious sense. The restrained use of such metaphors reinforces the link between the symbolic value of a hostile setting and suffering in narrative actuality. In such a setting, Dupas, a doubting priest, has travelled to a frontier where he can confront men in the throes of problems which might lead to God. He is seeking some advance on the meaningless small services which have hitherto been his only contact. A series of flashbacks shows Dupas as a young curate, already bewildered by the ecclesiastical view of human nature, and nursing in the depths of his humility an obscure revolt. Finding a moment in which he could not accept God's justice, he was repulsed by the inhuman detachment of his superior and left to seek his own way. The aim of the lonely hero was to seek God through men. He went to the forest (an odd choice for seeking men) because he wanted to make his contact with men natural, direct and authentic, as a man among men. He thought of lumberjacks as: "Des exemplaires d'hommes, sans camouflage, réduits à l'essentiel" (T 62), "une humanité brute." But he will be lost in their ambiguity. As the drama unfolds, he is able to perceive but not share the motives and reactions of the men around him. Perceptive even to the extent of annoying them, he is really as lost among amorous rivals as Sagard was among his first Hurons. He has rejected the code of human nature which his seminary training offered him, and finds that without a system he is helpless:

Au séminaire on lui avait enseigné l'homme, un homme qu'il cherchait encore. Quand il les avait connus, eux, le code qu'on lui avait donné pour mesurer les actes humains lui avait brûlé les mains. Il était resté démuni. [T 62]
Il était difficile et périlleux d'aimer dans la solitude, sans l'appui d'un système où tout était prévu. [T 90]

Unable to penetrate the hates and loves of his fellows, he finds himself reduced once more to small services. He will be a Martha again and stoke the wood-stove for them.

Ultimately, Dupas's rejection of system goes back to a rejection of original sin (T 143). Consequently, it may be said without exaggeration that Dupas has gone North to escape from the confines of a human nature predetermined by the doctrine of the Fall.

The presence of guests other than that of Dupas intensifies the forest journey of *Le Temps des hommes*. Maurice, the bastard cook, is looking for parents; he eventually finds his mother in the snow where he curls up to die. Gros Louis and his assassin are both looking for different kinds of freedom to love and be happy. Baptiste is a traditional French-Canadian farmer, absorbed in his family and property; yet even he was not there only for the money to buy a new tractor. These human searches will necessarily impinge on that of Dupas, the priest looking for God.

Both *Poussière sur la ville* and *Le Temps des hommes* furnish several other ways of putting human ambiguity both in dialogue and in action. The miners digging their graves to make a living, Dubois torn between helping his wife and attending to his patients, two kinds of love denoted by Gros Louis's sister and his mistress, and the resolution of what is obstensibly a spiritual problem by physical hunger and exposure, all these basic situations expand Langevin's vision of man torn between aspiration and limitation. These realities, and the thing in tension between them, constitute a human condition rather than a human nature. That is to say that Langevin's man is defined by his potentialities and limitations rather than by a set of fixed qualities.

Both Langevin's heroes, Dubois and Dupas, face a bleak world in which to sound this condition, and both come to the problem bearing the memory of a dead child. The crux of Dubois's interrogation of the elderly doctor Lafleur is that man cannot abstain from probing what appears to him to be a flaw in God's justice. He questions the serenity of his elder partner in face of suffering, and challenges our right to be happy with a Christian hope which does not answer man's questions: "Il n'a pas le droit de nous proposer son bonheur si cette pierre-là est disjointe" (P 127). Langevin's characters are looking for certainties which they can imagine but which the earth itself seems to deny. Dupas, because he is a priest, is less prepared than these doctors to find his answer in accepting "notre métier d'homme" (P 128) and "les moyens humains" (P 154). Yet these are in fact at the core of his problem, because he is trying to reconcile God and man with each other. The dialogue is transferred to his parish priest, Monseigneur Major, a competent administrator. This is a priest who has accepted the necessity of working on the human scale of the Church Militant, with a filing cabinet and a cash register. Yet under his hard exterior he is a disappointed man. He has the memory of past ambitions, and of a youthful idealism.

Monseigneur Major sortait un peu ahuri de sa course aux chiffres et, le matin à la messe, il devait songer lui aussi avec une secrète nostalgie à l'Eglise des catacombes. Les ans, l'habitude, l'avaient endurci. Peut-être avait-il oublié le jeune prêtre qu'il avait été. Il avait fait en somme une carrière de laïc au sein de l'Eglise. Quelque chose lui avait été dérobé en cours de route, de précieux, de vital, son âme de prêtre. Il ne fouettait tellement les jeunes prêtres qui lui étaient confiés que parce qu'ils lui rappelaient dans leur juvénile ardeur, dans leur désir maladroit d'absolue pureté, cette perte jamais reconnue. [T 153–54]

In the contrast between him and Dupas, we have two different ways of viewing the agonizing gulf between man's real means and his equally real aspirations.

Dupas's rejection of original sin is also found in *Poussière sur la ville* when the idea of absolute justice is opposed to cerebrospinal meningitis, the malady which kills a child in front of Dupas. Dupas, like Dr. Lafleur, accepts that this amounts to a belief in injustice, but he goes further, and agrees that it also amounts to a choice:

J'ai choisi l'enfant contre Dieu. Un prêtre choisit Dieu sans retour, Laurier. Moi, je me suis repris pour me donner à l'enfant. C'était comme si je n'avais plus été prêtre. Mon rôle était d'offrir ses souffrances à Dieu. Je n'ai pas accepté. [T 147]

His action throughout the novel is an attempt to justify this choice, by returning to God through men.

Il avait quitté un abri sûr et ancien, les murs du séminaire, pour mettre le pied dans l'univers exposé, démuni, des hommes. Pour une seconde il avait été de ce monde "dont nous ne sommes pas". . . . Cette paroi de verre qui le défendait depuis l'âge de raison il avait maintenant une impérieuse nécessité de la broyer. Changer de direction. Aller à Dieu par les hommes. Puisque par la tentation dans la chambre de l'enfant il s'était dépouillé de la dignité que ses supérieurs et Dieu lui avait confiée . . . il repartirait du niveau le plus humble, au pied des hommes. [T 155]

His two attempts to bridge the gap will fail. There is on the one hand no human method of preventing suffering and crime such as adultery and murder. Nor will it, finally, be possible to enter into possession of Laurier's baseness, to make it into some higher spiritual value which would justify man and God to each other. The expectation and failure of Dupas's quest are repeated several times, successively magnified. His work of direct, intelligible practical service to man continues, because through human goodness he expects to find the kindly God of his childhood *images d'Epinal*. Twice he fails to intervene between Laurier, a man who tries to possess his wife like a conquered prize, and Gros Louis, the wife's lover and the husband's foreman. The last and greatest of his hopes in salvation by good works is to stop Laurier from shooting Gros Louis.

Dupas realizes that the challenge to which he is now rising is all the more serious, because the jealous husband is asking for some essential contact with him as a man. Their long conversation forms a static and elusive climax, in which Laurier and Dupas exchange the rôles of saver and sinner back and forth as they pass the whisky bottle. Laurier both discovers that Dupas is a priest, and suggests that he has succeeded in being a man among men. Dupas is able to bow down and make his confession to a wretched sinner, having refused it all these years to his ecclesiastical superiors. He tells how he refused to accept suffering and explains (apparently for the first time) that he was thereby claiming to be more just than God. Here he is at last recognizing and purging the pride of which he had been accused. However, he is caught in a confusing dilemma. It is by accepting guilt that he makes himself recognizably a man; yet the guilt he accepts is, according to Laurier, special to priests. Furthermore, he commanded Laurier's respect so long as he was the arm of God; in becoming a man he must lose it, and with it some of his chance of doing good as a man. At moments during the reversal of rôles, the dialogue takes the form of Laurier plucking out God's iniquity, and later in the novel it is explicitly recognized that Dupas, in accepting the death of the child at last, has assumed

the guilt of God, and feels that he too is a murderer.[9] Laurier
continues to deny that Dupas can really feel the cares of a man,
heaping scorn on him for maintaining his celibacy, which has
caused the suffering of a young woman and sheltered the selfish
man from conjugal passions. Dupas slides from his uneasy
plateau, a failure both as man and God. The failure of the
Pelagian God is completed by the murder of Gros Louis, with
Dupas among the helpless witnesses.

Again he will rise from failure. This time the recovery is rapid.
Dupas has seen that the first stage of his quest has come full
circle. He assumes the spiritual quest, accepting his own condition outside the days of men, accepting the suffering and death
of the innocent, praying for the redemption of the murderer and
his adulterous victim through a mystery higher than human
justice. He has accepted Laurier's view of the situation, which
means accepting the rôle of an inhuman God, and accepting that
man is a born sinner whom he must save. From man seeking
God, he has become God seeking man.

A second search accompanies the physical journey round Le
Grand Lac Désert. It is the most arduous journey of all, and
worthy of all the missionary martyrs. The two men struggle,
without proper food, shelter or directions, through a terrible
blizzard, and experience the full gamut of attendant sufferings.
The hostility of the land, which has been present in all of the
preceding episodes, now steps boldly into the foreground. It is
the brutal evidence of a world in which there is incomprehensible
suffering. It is also the tangible image of human freedom as
Langevin sees it; Laurier, fleeing, thinks the forest offers him at
least enough liberty to play out his driving passion, but in fact
he is only free to die.

Dupas, intent on reaching this man's soul, follows him dog-
gedly, carrying first the pack and then the sinner. He is willing
to bear the sins of man and God alike, if he can now find justification. In a moment of lucidity the murderer realizes why the
priest needs him: this confession, this atonement, they are wanted
not only for him, but also for the God that permits innocents to
suffer. He will refuse to the very end:

[9]Dupas accepts Laurier's statement: "Tu dis que tu as tué un enfant"
(T 216).

Mon crime c'est à moi. Tu tournes autour de moi comme si tu voulais me l'arracher. Je le tiens bien. Je mourrai avant de te le passer. Et quelle sorte de confession? Y as-tu pensé? Comme je le comprends ce serait trop facile. Je me confesse. Je suis lavé et toi aussi. Ça ne peut pas être aussi facile que cela. [T 216]

The scene ends with a blizzard, as if the elements are joining in this denial of an ultimate redemption of God and man by each other.

As the struggle continues on the parallel planes of the argument and the journey, the details of the latter are intensified. Laurier, suffering from fatigue and pneumonia, clings at last to the priest, but he is clinging for life, not redemption. Dupas is still trying to share everything; he even lets the sick man breathe germs into his face. But it is an equivocal self-sacrifice. It may save him personally, but it does nothing for the ordinary men he wanted to redeem. Dupas, either as man or God, is still inadequate. The one moment when Laurier seeks Dupas—because he is afraid of men—is like an ugly parody of love, made of fear and cruelty. Finally, he rejects such a realizable deity, from whom he wanted only physical support in time of need: "je veux durer, durer. Toi, ça m'est égal" (T 222).

Dying of exposure to the harsh nature which has been present in the entire struggle, Laurier finally tries to shoot the man he identifies with God. This should not be taken merely as the aberration of a sick man, since it is consistent with his steadfast refusal to submit to either divine or human justice. In the ensuing struggle, it is Dupas who shoots Laurier. The author offers no comment and no dialogue to explain what this event signifies to him or the characters. The whole argument about what is elsewhere called divine injustice has been brought back from the realms of speculation to that of action. However, since he has now killed the unredeemed sinner, Dupas has evidently failed. Having abandoned the earlier attempt to find good men and a kindly God in the same place, he tried to be the link between a higher, sterner God and a lower, more despicable man (Laurier is an unpleasant character from beginning to end). He seems to have made contact with neither God nor man, because he has never made up his mind to be on one side or the other.

In a brief epilogue, again without comment, we see Dupas in

the hotel where the journey began, unconscious and severely frostbitten. Yolande, the thoroughly carnal woman, wife of the assassin and mistress of the victim, is looking at him for the first time as a man. In this gesture, Langevin offers the mocking suggestion that Dupas succeeded in entering the days of men by killing, just as he had returned to the priesthood by accepting guilt and death. It would be very hard to take this as a real success, a revindication of the doctrine of original sin. The higher justice which condones the suffering of children has not been understood by any character other than Laurier who rejected it and Dupas who cannot communicate it. The living are left with their unanswered question in a hostile universe.

Reference to *Poussière sur la ville* throws more light on this question. The character of Madeleine, as we have seen, represents the tragic pursuit of happiness in a freedom which does not exist. Her husband and the parish priest comment on her actions, and occasionally meet to argue about her. The priest, representative of a teleological system, brings her into a field of judgment involving duty, natural and divine laws, and an analysis which in the last resort separates the act from the agent: "Je ne condamne pas l'âme. Je condamne l'acte scandaleux" (P 162). Madeleine herself always seems to elude him. Dubois has formulated some natural laws of his own such as: "On ne peut avoir des droits sur un être qu'on ne peut empêcher de mourir" (P 152). He has situated the human problem in an absurd universe and established the criterion of happiness as the only certainty we possess. He accepts that this cannot lead him to any logically necessary conclusion. The priest, on the other hand, argues logically in a self-contained system: he can rationalize the absence of terrestrial happiness without stumbling over the human reality of it. In the view of Dubois he misses the real problem, just as in *Le Temps des hommes* Dupas feels that his own failure as a priest is an incapacity to give men something essential. Langevin's priests are protected from the world of men by a glass wall which is their theology, but which also suggests the impossibility of any real contact between the God they represent and the men they judge, control or serve.

Laurier's entire story is presented as a psychological reality. He is a violent, selfish man under his controlled exterior. He has learned control because people do not like him, and thanks to it managed to impress and marry a girl who was always ready to carry her unsatisfied dreams to the handsome lumberjack hero. Laurier insists, in telling the celibate Dupas what sexual passions are, that the triangle situation and his need for vengeance are like physical realities; to live as a man one cannot ignore them. Gros Louis, the lover, is also driven by emotional realities which we have to accept, and he brushes aside the *curé*'s suggestion that he should not leave the camp to see Yolande again. Under his assured exterior, he carries the hopeless love of a tubercular sister whom he cannot save. He finds relief in the immediate satisfactions offered by women like Yolande. The other characters in the camp bring equally "real" stories to add to the human reality sought but not embraced by Dupas. This is constantly echoed by the reality of the universe in the form of external nature, and linked with it in important narrative details such as the difficulties of travel and communication.

At times the physical realities of the narrative lead directly into the metaphysical theme, without losing any of their force as direct human sufferings. The dying child's inability to take a communion wafer from Dupas is an involuntary rejection of the formal symbol of godhead closely connected with Dupas's own revolt:

Il ne réussit pas à faire avaler l'hostie à l'enfant.
La langue gonflée la repoussait dans un râle.
La mère, les yeux illuminés, disait patiemment:
—Avale le bon Dieu, Jean. Avale le bon Dieu.
Mais l'enfant était depuis longtemps hors d'atteinte.
—Avale le bon Dieu, Jean. Avale le bon Dieu.
—Epargnez l'innocent. Mon Dieu, je vous demande la guérison. . . .
Il demandait avec violence, tout son corps tendu vers l'hostie qu'il essayait de remettre dans la bouche de l'enfant. [T 135]

. . . .

[Dupas comments to Laurier] —Alors, vois-tu ce que j'ai fait? J'ai nié la rédemption. J'ai dit à Dieu: les souffrances de l'enfant sont inutiles, il est pur et vous le torturez en vain. Je ne crois plus en la rédemption, je crois à l'injustice. [T 147]

It is particularly striking that Dupas has not formulated his revolt intellectually, he is merely commenting on an experience which he accepts like a physical necessity he would rather have overcome. Meanwhile, the agony of the child and his mother continue on one plane of action, Laurier's resentment and criminal plans on another. Man, abandoned to his crimes, incapable of solving his own sufferings or of accepting the comfort of doctrines, will go on struggling and discussing. For he is equally unable to give up the search, the endless question which Job addressed to God. It is in this framework that the art of Langevin makes human experience into the loudest human protest.

The material which has so far been related to the theme of metaphysical revolt indicates at once a protest on the speculative level, mainly concentrated in the challenging of God, and a protest arising directly from "real" situations in the narrative. There is also a level of social protest. This is much more evident in Langevin's first novel, *Evadé de la nuit*, still very violent in *Poussière sur la ville*, and decidedly secondary in *Le Temps des hommes*, the author's third and possibly last novel. However, it is of more significance to note that the three levels of protest are all present, and indissoluble from each other. Langevin's is a creation which makes its own unity. The various types of significance emanate from it in their place, but without any evident system that could be compared with the methodical satire of, say, André Giroux's *Au delà des visages*.

The protest against society parallels the description of places. Asbestos-bearing regions are bleak, the pulpwood forest is depressing and cruel: the people of Macklin and the Scott Power and Paper Company, respectively, have produced human environments of equivalent monstrosity. The protest is largely against society as an inhuman creation; there is no straying into the special social and political problems of the French-Canadian people. The Establishment is best typified by Monseigneur Major. He is concerned for the spiritual direction of the prosperous Sacred Heart league, but dismisses as a drunkard the father of the dead child. Dupas feels like an outcast with his sympathy for a man broken by suffering. There is the same difference between the money-grubbers of Macklin, and Dubois's attempt to see suffering with pity and charity.

Arthur Prévost, proprietor of the general store and high priest of personal property, is the real conscience of the people of Macklin. He is helpful, affable, and has the interest of the community at heart. To help Dubois, and also to secure his services for Macklin, he offers a loan at less than the bank rate. But on the other side of these virtues is a harsh, narrow public conscience. He assumes the right to moralize, without question, on account of his generosity. Here he is explicitly speaking for the town: "Dans une ville comme Macklin, vous ne pouvez avoir de vie privée" (P 132). The whole town assumes that, because it is ultimately supporting Dubois, it must dictate to him and his wife an exact code of behaviour. Since this tyranny is principally what suffocates Madeleine, the plot of this novel contains a very eloquent social argument. It opposes society's right to make its own values cardinal, with a kind of utilitarian argument based on the measurement of individual happiness.

The absence of any wider argument on the social plane and of any active sympathy for society as a necessary form may be attributed to the general character of *pays d'en haut* inspiration. When, at the end of the novel, Dubois returns to Macklin intent on securing its love for Madeleine, he is accepting humanity rather than society. This is somewhat different from Camus's Rieux and Rambert choosing not to escape from Oran when it is sealed for the plague. The *pays d'en haut* setting tends to reduce social problems to the simple argument of individual versus rule. It is a tendency towards abstraction rather than nuance. Some exception is to be found in Yves Thériault's visions of society engaged in the same implacable struggle as the individual, or Bertrand Vac's sympathetic portrayal of a woman escaping from village life.

Nevertheless, some feeling of social protest is always present, particularly if Langevin's three novels are considered as a whole. In *Poussière sur la ville* Madeleine and her husband are driven to seek escape from the rigid little society in which they live. In *Le Temps des hommes* Dupas has left society in order to become a man. There is a sequence, and if we go back to *Evadé de la nuit* we find a repressive society represented by a paralytic judge cursing his daughter. This figure is continued in the priest who condemns Madeleine and in the superior who lays down an unfeeling practical law to Dupas. Eventually, Langevin was drawn fully into the *pays d'en haut* setting to express his escape. This setting brings the characters into direct confrontation with

God, including God's law-making aspect. Langevin's characters flee or attempt to flee beyond the frontier of society when they find its laws are stronger than its compassion.

It is this sense of the fugitive that links Langevin's novels most deeply to the entire *pays d'en haut* tradition. Life beyond the pale is expected to be fuller and freer, just as it was in the missionaries' view of the happy savages and in the *coureurs de bois*'s personal and commercial ambitions. When Laurier discovers the guilt which binds Dupas to himself, he thinks of them both on equal terms as two fugitives into the forest. Their spiritual adventure could never be fully played out in any setting other than the boundless forest.

Other vestiges of the tradition are visible in *Le Temps des hommes*. Langevin's lumberjacks are less colourful, perhaps, than those of Joseph-Charles Taché, but there are many similarities besides the fact of being outlaws. The canoes are gone, but the arduous journey undertaken by hardy men in savage scenery remains. The special skills of the forest are less prominent but still there. Folk songs and tales have been replaced by obscene photographs, but in a time of tension, Laurier is found carving his axe handle in the form of a moose's head whose bare teeth express his rage. The journey linked to the spiritual quest is an adaptation of spiritual journeys such as those of Alfred Des-Rochers and Gabrielle Roy. It is often interrupted, or fades away under the long dialogues, but the journey provides a necessary framework and contains the hunger, fatigue, exposure and blizzards which successive French-Canadian writers have associated with escape, search, purification and regeneration. Dupas's —and Langevin's—choice of the forest as a place to look for human nature is entirely illogical and can only be explained by a literary tradition which amounts in fact to a long-standing myth.

In view of what his search actually finds, Langevin's use of the myth could be regarded as a deliberate reversal of tradition. Macklin, too, is the opposite of the freedom we expect in the *pays d'en haut*. There is in fact considerable use of anti-tradition comparable with that of Ringuet and Roger Lemelin. Just as the lover in *Poussière sur la ville* was a complete failure as a virile lumberjack hero, the dutiful farmer in *Le Temps des hommes* is a failure as the solid mainstay of traditional morality. Jean-Baptiste—the name declares Langevin's intention—is faithful to institutions including marriage, and loyal to the boss whatever he does. The moral conflict which the boss's adultery brings him is solved by the simple expedient of refusing to face the facts. He is completely absorbed in clearing his land, working for a new tractor and looking after his family. These domestic virtues are not enough. The one man strong enough to take Laurier's pistol and avert tragedy, he spends the most critical time in a drunken stupor and is eventually shot because he has not enough imagination to see what is going on. The physical description of Baptiste shows a man who is all sinew, with a small head.

Besides its value as a deliberate reversal of the *Jean Rivard* tradition, the presence of Baptiste underlines Langevin's attitude to moral responsibility. Baptiste fails and is killed through lack of involvement with his fellow men and failure to assume any responsibility for them. His virtues are all contained in the narrow circle of his wife's petticoats. His deferral of all responsibility to established authority continues in the exaggerated respect he shows for the boss even when the latter is dead. He is a foil to the typical Langevin characters, Dubois, Dupas, Laurier, who are all trying to gain their own freedom, and with it to build a humanity such as they envisage. Their idea of responsibility is like that of the French existentialists, whereas his is purely hierarchical.

The rejection of traditional atittudes and beliefs, a favourite topic of Ringuet and a central question for Yves Thériault, is, then, an integral part of Langevin's revolt. It is also visible in Gabrielle Roy, whose ironic view of the farmer's self-sufficiency in *Alexandre Chenevert* sets the limit on Alexandre's claim to have discovered happiness. Here, as in *Le Temps des hommes*, the special Canadian rebellion joins in the essential unity of the different planes of revolt. For the confused worries that assail Alexandre, jostling and engendering each other, are not merely an imitation of an ordinary man's stream of consciousness. Alexandre struggles for an order which he can never establish. His worries really are all related to each other, in defiance of classification. The solution found in his journey is a solution to all of them. Langevin's fusion of the different planes of interest is more to be seen in his difficult structures. *Le Temps des hommes* breaks chronological sequence to superimpose on each other the spiritual crisis of Dupas at a child's death-bed, the subsequent dialogue between Dupas and his senior, the latter's own moments of doubt at the height of a successful ministry, and finally, Laurier's conception, execution, and expiation of the murder of Gros Louis. In this arrangement, spiritual, moral, personal and physical suffering are brought together under the essential unity of the novel.

The accumulated associations of a journey which is a deep personal quest, of a challenging new view of human beings arising from new discoveries, and of the continued physical presence of geographical regions which can be regarded as a polyvalent frontier—these memories are like a nucleus of reality to all the disturbances that give rise to protest. The protest can take the shape of a vital exultation or a more deliberate attack on the restraints of society and its cherished beliefs. Combining these forces, it produces an assertion of man against his invincible cosmic misfortunes. All these developments draw their libertine spirit from a direct contact with one of the frontier regions, whatever intellectual debt they may have to contemporary French writers. Although the original *coureurs de bois* may have been mere naughty boys, the happy savages mere men, and the prospect of rich discoveries partly a delusion, awareness of the *pays d'en haut* remained as a living force after their historical importance had ended. Freed from the bounds of actuality, this awareness has grown into a more complete, more audacious, and finally a more spiritual liberation.

Conclusion

The recurrence of certain features in widely differing literary works leads to the question of a collective contribution in individual artistic creations. Interest in this question has at various times and in various schools of thought concentrated on different elements: artistic rules, moral situations, the message, or structures variously defined. Communication demands that there be something shared between a writer and his readers, but it is one of the characteristics of creative literature that the something shared eludes simple definition. The great theories which have been produced usually seem to present one important aspect of a more complex whole. The collective part has a special importance in discussions of French-Canadian literature, if only because the question most often asked, whether there is indeed a French-Canadian literature, seeks to ascertain and describe such a part. There is, after that, the question of relating it to other collectivities with comparable expressions.

The present work has no such pretensions, but two points of departure suggest themselves. One is the Frontier in American literature, and the other is what Martin Turnell has called the French Dialogue between order and freedom. But these are two different orders of critical concept, and if they are both present in one sort of material we are led to support a very traditional view of literary studies. This is that they must be primarily literary. They will always need the help of analytical methods from other disciplines: psychology, geography, sociology, philology and so on. But the value of these is best recognized by their ability to meet each other in specific texts.

The French-Canadian themes connected with the *pays d'en haut* have been preserved, modified and transmitted by a great variety of individual writers. A common fund of imagery has meant different things at different moments, and conveyed ideas which are sometimes even in contradiction with each other. As a whole it has a certain coherence which is not in an unbroken continuity, not in a body of doctrine, not in an identical way of feeling, not even in a uniform use of vocabulary or exact choice of décor, but never far away from all these. This whole has expanded a portion of social history into legend, a legend enlarged by the most mediocre as well as the most distinguished writers who have drawn on it. Yet its most fruitful application, the growth of rebelliousness into serious revolt, depends on demystification. The dialogue between legend and realism has been essential to the process in which a geographical notion, impinging on a state of moral tension, helps it to find a substantial expression of its own.

Original sin and personal salvation, often against a background of moral turpitude or complacency, form a prominent axis in the best of the novels under consideration. Other important works are concerned with the collective assertion of a superior nature. In either case, the action usually moves away from society, to be played out in some desolation where the main character is alone with the cosmos, shaking his fist either in the face of or on behalf of a God whose presence is more palpable there. And in either case, it is evident that the God of this cosmos did not intend French Canadians to be comfortable.

For French-Canadian writers responding to North-American geography, historical associations bring their own special emphases: the ambiguity of human nature, awareness of the collective struggle and with it the conflict of cultural identity and individual freedom. The contribution of modern French fiction has been absorbed, with its ponderings on freedom and responsibility, the futility of human communication and the urgent but hopeless need to comprehend an inhuman universe. The result is a distinctive contribution to the literature of human protest, owing its expression partly to an accumulated awareness which can properly be ascribed to the French-Canadian heritage.

Vitality and freedom are two sectors of interest which are inseparable from the *pays d'en haut* and allied themes. They are most commonly united through a vision of natural man as the possessor of wholeness. This may turn out to be illusory, but its loss is felt to be real. There is great variety in the way these qualities materialize in the works of different authors: freedom can be obtained either through or in spite of cultural groups; vitality can be sexual, artistic, moral, geographical or other. Over these differences we can make the generalization that the French-Canadian writer looks to the *pays d'en haut* for a man who is whole, natural, vigourous and free.

Vitality, often expressed as virility or "hard" savageness, is found to be necessary to the good life in spite of its disruptive features. It is also necessary for the well being of society seen as the triumphant ethic or the spiritual empire. Pictures of physical prowess have to be attached to the spreading of religion. A hero who can kill a man and break laws can also convert men in the name of a higher law. The farmer needs the *coureur de bois*, and without the libertine the city would be a necropolis. Stagnation and corruption are felt to be the dangers of moral stability, and must be met with an audacity that can only exist in freedom. Without such audacity, religion, love and art become impotent. With it, on the other hand, come disorders which social organization seeks to avoid, and the pure libertine heads for self-destruction. This is the dilemma in which French-Canadian man is situated by his authors, whether they lean to one or the other side, or recoil from choice in loud protest. It is a dilemma which cannot be resolved, apparently, in theology or philosophy or politics, so the search for wholeness is projected into literature. Literature has at various times been a main outlet for freedom and vitality.

Within French-Canadian literature the *pays d'en haut* have a history of their own, with ups and downs according to the varying needs for a rebel expression. Its major inconsistencies amount to a quasi-systematic dialogue between individualized and centralized visions of self-fulfilment. The latter is strongly marked by reaction to the minority situation, the former by reaction to paternalism. The theme also has an ancestry beyond the minority situation, though this is not an unbroken continuity. There are distinct resemblances between early travellers' reactions to the journey *en haut* and those of modern writers. There are distinct profiles in modern literature of a human nature envisaged by

the Frenchmen of the Counter-Reformation. The French Canadians are the descendants of those *libertins*, churchmen, adventurers and bureaucrats who tried to possess a vast continent with
a few thousand men. Their writers are apt to put their questions
about the human condition in certain ways, among which the
flight into the bush is striking because it is non-rational. Jansenist
attitudes seem to flourish in this atmosphere, but it must be
emphasized that that does not constitute proof of historical continuity on the plane of religious thought. Jansenist attitudes are
not very noticeable in the works of the early missionaries or of
their nineteenth-century emulators. The size of their collective
problem and their need for optimism about human nature
inclined them more towards Molinism. The "Jansenism" of
modern Montrealers probably owes less to subversive literature
spread (allegedly) by Frontenac than to adjustment to the
capitalist society of the nineteenth century. But their spiritual
solitudes have found expression in the remembered physical solitudes which form the starting point of this book. What has
survived from the past, neither intact nor unrecognizable, is a
rebel type in a legendary world strong enough to persist through
successive literary and ideological fashions.

Fidelity to that memory appears to be a condition of success
in making a convincing literary expression of the *pays d'en haut*.
Even the most painstaking application of local colour can fail to
provide conviction. One has the impression that the best writers
on this theme are *coureurs de bois manqués*. The traditional
material they use and their personal reflections upon it are fully
in possession of each other. The *pays d'en haut* at their best are
a state of mind into which the boldest spirits can run to seek
their self-completion.

BIBLIOGRAPHY

1(a). LITERARY WORKS CENTRAL TO THE THEME

DESROCHERS, ALFRED. *A l'Ombre de l'Orford.* Montreal: Librairie d'Action Canadienne-française, 1930.

DESROSIERS, LÉO-PAUL. *Les Engagés du Grand Portage.* Paris: Gallimard, 1938.

GRANDBOIS, *Alain. Né à Québec . . .; Louis Jolliet; récit.* Paris: Albert Messein, 1933.

LANGEVIN, ANDRÉ. *Poussière sur la ville.* 2nd ed. Paris: Laffont, 1955.

———— *Le Temps des hommes.* Montreal: Le Cercle du Livre de France, 1956.

LEMELIN, ROGER. *Pierre le magnifique.* Paris: Flammarion, 1953.

PANNETON, PHILIPPE (pseud. RINGUET). *Fausse monnaie.* Montreal: Editions Variétés, 1947.

———— *Un Monde était leur empire.* Montreal: Editions Variétés, 1943.

PELLETIER, AIMÉ (pseud. BERTRAND VAC). *Louise Genest.* Montreal: Le Cercle du Livre de France, 1950.

RINGUET. See Panneton, Philippe.

ROY, GABRIELLE. *Alexandre Chenevert.* Montreal: Beauchemin, 1954.

———— *La Montagne secrète.* Montreal: Beauchemin, 1961.

SAGARD, GABRIEL. *Le Grand Voyage du pays des Hurons*, ed. G. M. Wrong with trans. as *The Long Journey to the Country of the Hurons.* 3rd ed. Toronto: The Champlain Society, 1939.

TACHÉ, JOSEPH-CHARLES. *Forestiers et voyageurs*, ed. Luc Lacourcière. 2nd ed. Montreal: Fides, 1946.

THÉRIAULT, YVES. *Agaguk.* Quebec: Institut littéraire, 1958.

———— *Ashini.* Montreal: Fides, 1960.

———— *Cul-de-sac.* Quebec: Institut littéraire, 1961.

VAC, BERTRAND. See Pelletier, Aimé.

1(b). OTHER WORKS RELATED TO THE THEME

BARBEAU, MARIUS. *Le Rêve de Kamalmouk.* Montreal: Fides, 1948.

BERNARD, HARRY. *Les Jours sont longs.* Montreal: Le Cercle du Livre de France, 1951.

BREYNAT, GABRIEL. *Cinquante Ans au pays des neiges.* Trilogy: I *Chez les Mangeurs de caribou,* II *Voyageur du Christ,* III *L'Evêque volant.* Montreal: Fides, 1945, 1947, 1948.

BUCHAN, JOHN. *Sick Heart River.* Toronto: Musson, 1941.

CHAPMAN, WILLIAM. *Les Aspirations.* Paris: Librairies-imprimeries réunies Motteray, Martinet, 1904.

CHOPIN, RENÉ. *Le Cœur en exil.* Paris: Georges Crès, 1913.

DESROSIERS, LÉO-PAUL. *Nord-Sud.* Montreal: Editions du *Devoir,* 1931.

——— *Les Opiniâtres.* Montreal: Eds. du *Devoir,* 1941.

——— *Sources.* Montreal: Imprimerie populaire, 1942.

DUGAS(T), G. *Un Voyageur des pays d'en haut.* 2nd ed. Montreal: Beauchemin, 1912.

——— *La Première Canadienne du Nord-Ouest; ou Biographie de Marie-Anne Gaboury, arrivée au Nord-Ouest en 1806 et décédée à Saint-Boniface à l'âge de 96 ans.* Montreal: Librairie Saint-Joseph, Cadieux & Derome, 1883.

FRÉCHETTE, LOUIS. *La Légende d'un peuple.* Paris: Librairie illustrée, 1887.

GARNEAU, H. DE SAINT-DENYS. *Journal.* Montreal: Beauchemin, 1954.

GÉRIN-LAJOIE. *Jean Rivard le defricheur.* 4th ed. Montreal: Beauchemin, 1925.

GRIGNON, CLAUDE-HENRI. *Un Homme et son péché.* Montreal: Eds. du Totem, 1933.

GUÈVREMONT, GERMAINE (née GRIGNON). *Le Survenant.* Montreal: Beauchemin, 1945.

HÉMON, LOUIS. *Maria Chapdelaine; Récit du Canada français.* Fayard ed. Paris: Fayard, 1935.

HUBERT-ROBERT, RÉGINE. *L'Epopée de la fourrure.* Montreal: Editions de l'Arbre, 1945.

MACLENNAN, HUGH. *The Watch that Ends the Night.* Toronto: Macmillan, 1959.

PANNETON, PHILIPPE (pseud. RINGUET). *Trente Arpents.* 2nd ed. Montreal: Fides, 1957.

PASCAL, BLAISE. *Œuvres complètes.* Paris: Gallimard (Pléiade 34), 1962.

RINGUET. See Panneton, Philippe.

ROY, GABRIELLE. *La Petite Poule d'Eau.* Montreal: Beauchemin, 1950.

——— *Rue Deschambault.* Montreal: Beauchemin, 1955.

SAINT-DENYS GARNEAU. See Garneau, H. de Saint-Denys.

SAVARD, FÉLIX-ANTOINE. *L'Abatis* (*version définitive*). Montreal: Fides, 1960.

—— *Menaud, maître-draveur*. 3rd ed. Montreal: Fides, 1960.

TACHÉ, ALEXANDRE-ANTONIN. *Esquisse sur le Nord-Ouest de l'Amérique*. Montreal: Charles Peyette, 1869.

—— *Vingt Années de missions dans le Nord-Ouest de l'Amérique*. 2nd ed. Montreal: Cadieux & Derome, 1888.

THÉRIAULT, YVES. *Le Dompteur d'ours*. Montreal: Le Cercle du Livre de France, 1951.

1(c). RECOMMENDED ANTHOLOGIES

FOURNIER, JULES. *Anthologie des poètes canadiens*. Montreal: Granger frères, 1920.

RIÈSE, LAURE. *L'Ame de la poésie canadienne-française*. Toronto: Macmillan, 1955.

2. HISTORICAL AND CRITICAL WORKS

Archives coloniales: *Canada, Correspondance générale, C 11 A*. Volumes 3–6, 33, 35. Paris.

BERR, HENRI. *Du scepticisme de Gassendi*. Trad. Bernard Rochot. Paris: Albin Michel, 1960.

BRYMNER, DOUGLAS. *Report on Canadian Archives, 1886*. Ottawa, 1887.

BUIES, ARTHUR. *Le Saguenay et le bassin du lac Saint-Jean; ouvrage historique et descriptif*. 3rd ed. Quebec: Brousseau, 1896.

CHAMPLAIN, SAMUEL DE. *The Works of Samuel de Champlain*. 6 vols. Toronto: The Champlain Society, 1922–1935.

CHARLEVOIX. *Histoire et description generale de la Nouvelle France, avec le Journal historique d'un voyage fait par ordre du roi dans l'Amérique septentrionale*. 3 vols. Paris: Nyon fils, 1744.

CHINARD, GILBERT. *L'Amérique et le rêve exotique dans la littérature française au XVIIe et au XVIIIe siècle*. Paris: Droz, 1934.

—— *L'Exotisme américain dans la littérature française au XVIe siècle d'après Rabelais, Ronsard, Montaigne etc*. Paris: Hachette, 1911.

CIRLOT, J. E. *A Dictionary of Symbols*, trans. Jack Sage. London: Routledge & Kegan Paul, 1962.

CRUICKSHANK, JOHN. *Albert Camus and the Literature of Revolt*. 2nd ed. New York: O.U.P., 1960.

DANTIN, LOUIS. See Seers, Eugène.

GROULX, LIONEL. *Histoire du Canada français*. 2nd ed., 3 vols. Montreal: Action nationale, 1951.

HARPER, GEORGE MC LEAN. *The Legend of the Holy Grail*, reprinted from the Publications of the Modern Language Association of America, N.S. I, No. 1. Baltimore: MLA, 1893.

HAZARD, PAUL. *La Crise de la conscience européenne (1680–1715)*. 3 vols. Paris: Boivin, 1935.

JUNG, C. G. *Contributions to Analytical Psychology*. London: Routledge and Kegan Paul, 1928.

LAFLÈCHE, LOUIS-FRANÇOIS. *Quelques Considérations sur les rapports de la société civile avec la religion et la famille*. Montreal: Sénécal, 1866.

LÉGARÉ, ROMAIN. *L'Aventure poétique et spirituelle de Saint-Denys Garneau*. Montreal: Fides, 1957.

LOVEJOY, ARTHUR O., GEORGE BOAS, and others. *Primitivism and Related Ideas in Antiquity*. Baltimore: Johns Hopkins Press, 1935.

MORICE, A-G *Dictionnaire historique des Canadiens et des Métis français de l'Ouest*. Quebec: Laflamme et Proulx, 1908.

MOWAT, FARLEY. *People of the Deer*. London: Michael Joseph, 1952.

NUTE, GRACE LEE. *The Voyageur*. New York: Appleton, 1931.

SEERS, EUGÈNE (pseud. LOUIS DANTIN). *Gloses critiques* (second series). Montreal: Lévesque, 1934.

TURNELL, MARTIN. *The Novel in France*. 2nd ed. New York: Vintage, 1958.

3. ARTICLES IN PERIODICALS

CHINARD, GILBERT. "Influence des récits de voyage sur la philosophie de J-J Rousseau," *Publications of the Modern Languages Association of America*, XXVI N.S. XIX (1911), 476–95.

GARNEAU, RENÉ. "Du Concept de la littérature au Canada," *La Nouvelle Revue canadienne*, I, 1 (février-mars, 1951), 15–26.

ROBINSON, J. LEWIS. "Arctic Resources," *The Beaver*, Spring, 1959, 9–11.

WHALLEY, GEORGE. "Coppermine Martyrdom," *Queen's Quarterly*, LXVI (1959), 591–610.

Index